Department of Commerce and Labor

Annual report of the Commissioner-General of Immigration

Department of Commerce and Labor

Annual report of the Commissioner-General of Immigration

ISBN/EAN: 9783741140853

Manufactured in Europe, USA, Canada, Australia, Japa

Cover: Foto ©Suzi / pixelio.de

Manufactured and distributed by brebook publishing software
(www.brebook.com)

Department of Commerce and Labor

Annual report of the Commissioner-General of Immigration

ANNUAL REPORT

OF THE

COMMISSIONER-GENERAL OF IMMIGRATION

TO THE

SECRETARY OF COMMERCE AND LABOR

FOR THE

FISCAL YEAR ENDED JUNE 30, 1906

WASHINGTON
GOVERNMENT PRINTING OFFICE
1906

DEPARTMENT OF COMMERCE AND LABOR

Document No. 68

BUREAU OF IMMIGRATION AND NATURALIZATION

2

ANNUAL REPORT

OF THE

COMMISSIONER-GENERAL OF IMMIGRATION.

DEPARTMENT OF COMMERCE AND LABOR,
BUREAU OF IMMIGRATION AND NATURALIZATION,
Washington, July 1, 1906.

SIR: When it was announced at the close of the fiscal year 1905 that 1,026,499 aliens had entered the United States during the preceding twelve months, the opinion was expressed by many that the maximum had been reached in this peaceful invasion of the country by foreign peoples. The immigration for the said year exceeded that of the preceding by 213,629, and that of the year ended June 30, 1903, by 169,453. But the fiscal year just closed has produced a record eclipsing all former figures on this subject; for during said period the population of the United States has been increased by the admission of 1,100,735 immigrant aliens, and 65,618 nonimmigrant aliens (a segregation, not heretofore employed, explained in detail on page 4 of this report) have entered at its ports, making the total admissions 1,166,353. The increase over last year's record of 1,059,755 (1,026,499 aliens plus 33,256 transits) therefore is 106,598. During the fiscal year 1905, 11,480 aliens were rejected, and during the past year 12,432, an increase of 952. Hence the total number of those who have sought admission in 1906, viz, 1,178,785, exceeds the number applying in 1905, 1,071,235, by 107,550. Not alone in these respects, but also as to the amount and quality of the work performed, have the twelve months to a brief recital of the occurrences of which this report is addressed been the banner year in the history of the United States Immigration Service. The truth of this assertion must, it is believed, be admitted by all who give careful consideration to the tables and accompanying statement of facts herewith submitted, as compared with former reports of the Bureau.

In order that the various subjects covered may be presented clearly and concisely, they are classed under systematic and natural titles and subtitles, arranged in regular sequence, and for the sake of convenience indicated by Roman and Arabic numerals, respectively. Being of the greatest magnitude and importance of the several branches of the Bureau's work, the first subject to engage attention is

I. IMMIGRATION.

A comprehension of the principal figures regarding this subject is essential to the understanding of what follows in this report; therefore the various statistical tables and charts are inserted at this point and briefly discussed.

1. Statistical Tables and Charts.

It will be noted that the headings of several tables presented this year differ from those of tables bearing similar numerical designations included in former reports of the Bureau. This is due to the inauguration of the change, already alluded to, in the system of keeping the data from which the tables are compiled, the object being to make an accurate showing with regard to the number of aliens actually added to our population. In the year 1905 all aliens arriving at ports of this country, with the exception of those merely in transit to other countries, were reported as alien arrivals. During the fiscal year 1906 there have been segregated from those arriving, not only the transits, but all aliens returning from visits abroad to resume previously established permanent domiciles in the United States, and all coming simply as visitors or tourists with the intention of returning to homes abroad. It will be seen, therefore, that the total 1,100,735, so frequently appearing in the tables herewith presented, includes only what are termed "immigrant" aliens, i. e., those who intend to settle here. Also that the difference between those figures and 1,026,499, the total for 1905, viz, 74,236, does not give an accurate idea of the increase, but such accurate idea must be secured by adding to the figures for the present year those covering the number of nonimmigrant aliens arriving, viz, 65,618 (see Table XV, p. 46), making a total for comparative purposes of 1,166,353, and by adding to the figures for 1905 the number of aliens who during that year passed through in transit to other countries, viz, 33,256, making a total for comparative purposes of 1,059,755. By subtracting these two totals the difference between the work of inspecting aliens during the fiscal years 1905 and 1906 is obtained—a balance of 106,598 in favor of the last year, or an increase of about 10 per cent. Even this does not furnish a complete representation of the inspection work accomplished by officers of this service, for in addition there was examined an indeterminate number of passengers who claimed to be American citizens. Of this class 135,959 landed at the port of New York alone, and varying but much smaller numbers landed at the other large ports. (See Table XVI, p. 49.)

Table I gives a comparison, by ports of entry, between the number of aliens admitted during the year just closed and during the year ended June 30, 1905. It will be noted that while New York shows a gain of 91,817, the six ports next in importance as to numbers—Boston, Baltimore, Philadelphia, Honolulu, Key West, and San Francisco—each record a considerable reduction. The entire number representing the increase for the year, therefore, as well as a considerable portion of the number representing the losses at the other large ports, is included in the figures covering the increase at New York and in the slight increases at some of the smaller ports, the most striking of which is the gain of 3,434 made by Galveston, which, however, so far as that part of the country is concerned, is almost offset by a loss of nearly 2,000 at New Orleans.

TABLE I.—IMMIGRANT ALIENS ADMITTED INTO THE UNITED STATES, BY PORTS, DURING THE FISCAL YEARS ENDED JUNE 30, 1905 AND 1906.

Port.	1905.			1906.		
	Males.	Females.	Total.	Males.	Females.	Total.
New York, N. Y	553,084	235,135	788,219	608,647	271,389	880,036
Boston, Mass	38,460	26,647	65,107	37,943	24,286	62,229
Baltimore, Md	47,638	14,676	62,314	39,843	14,221	54,064
Philadelphia, Pa	15,224	8,600	23,824	14,117	9,069	23,186
San Francisco, Cal	5,332	1,045	6,377	3,388	750	4,138
San Juan, P. R	1,167	427	1,594	1,017	435	1,452
Bangor, Me	27	....	27	10	....	10
Brownsville, Tex	....	....	....	37	18	55
Brunswick, Ga	15	....	15	11	....	11
Douglas, Ariz	43	3	46	16	....	16
Eagle Pass, Tex	186	71	257	117	23	140
El Paso, Tex	704	129	833	1,388	280	1,668
Fernandina, Fla	3	....	3	3	....	3
Galveston, Tex	1,861	906	2,767	4,611	1,590	6,201
Gulfport, Miss	127	4	131	21	....	21
Honolulu, Hawaii	10,794	1,203	11,997	8,550	830	9,380
Jacksonville, Fla	13	4	17	17	3	20
Ketchikan, Alaska	4	1	5	65	8	73
Key West, Fla	5,597	2,491	8,088	3,688	1,631	5,319
Laredo, Tex	685	145	830	544	127	671
Miami, Fla	274	129	403	419	180	599
Mobile, Ala	241	67	308	245	47	292
Naco, Ariz	209	1	210	188	2	190
New Bedford, Mass	1,354	844	2,198	1,233	761	1,994
New Orleans, La	2,842	1,158	4,000	1,456	595	2,051
Nogales, Ariz	78	6	84	27	5	32
Norfolk, Va	159	6	165	47	9	56
Pensacola, Fla	129	....	129	56	....	56
Portland, Me	401	167	568	496	318	814
Portland, Oreg	38	3	41	....	....	....
Providence, R. I	....	....	....	17	2	19
Savannah, Ga	19	....	19	24	2	26
Seattle, Wash	1,541	164	1,705	1,627	289	1,916
Tucson, Ariz	4	....	4	....	....	....
Total United States	688,253	294,032	982,285	729,868	326,870	1,056,738
Through Canada via—						
Atlantic ports }	33,493	7,083	40,576	....	....	17,233
Border ports }				....	....	24,741
Pacific ports	3,168	470	3,638	....	....	2,023
Total Canada	36,661	7,553	44,214	34,595	9,402	43,997
Grand total	724,914	301,585	1,026,499	764,463	336,272	1,100,735

The tendency of immigration during the past few years to gather its steady increase principally from the countries of southern and eastern Europe is illustrated in a rather startling manner by Table II. Without exception, the countries from which we formerly obtained the greater part of our foreign population, and which are inhabited by races nearly akin to our own, have supplied us with smaller numbers during the past year than during 1905—Ireland 17,950, England 15,218, Sweden 3,281, Germany 3,010, Denmark 1,229, and Scotland 1,111 less. On the other hand, the four most considerable gains are: Italy, 51,641; Russia, 30,768; Greece, 8,974, and Turkey (in Europe and Asia), 5,165. These are significant figures and deserve careful study. The question, from what racial sources the blood is drawn that is being constantly injected into the veins of our own race, is more accurately answered, however, by the first four columns of Table III.

TABLE II.—IMMIGRATION INTO THE UNITED STATES DURING THE FISCAL YEARS ENDED JUNE 30, 1905 AND 1906, SHOWING INCREASE AND DECREASE FOR EACH COUNTRY.

Country of last permanent residence.	1905.	1906.	Increase (+) or decrease (−).
Austria-Hungary	275,693	265,138	−10,555
Belgium	5,302	5,099	− 203
Bulgaria, Servia, and Montenegro	2,043	4,666	+ 2,623
Denmark	8,970	7,741	− 1,229
France, including Corsica	10,168	9,386	− 782
German Empire	40,574	37,564	− 3,010
Greece	10,515	19,489	+ 8,974
Italy, including Sicily and Sardinia	221,479	273,120	+51,641
Netherlands	4,954	4,946	− 8
Norway	25,064	21,730	− 3,334
Portugal, including Cape Verde and Azore islands	5,028	8,517	+ 3,489
Roumania	4,437	4,476	+ 39
Russian Empire and Finland	184,897	215,665	+30,768
Spain, including Canary and Balearic islands	2,600	1,921	− 679
Sweden	26,591	23,310	− 3,281
Switzerland	4,269	3,846	− 423
Turkey in Europe	4,542	9,510	+ 4,968
United Kingdom:			
England	64,709	49,491	−15,218
Ireland	52,945	34,995	−17,950
Scotland	16,977	15,866	− 1,111
Wales	2,503	1,841	− 662
Other Europe	13	[illegible]	+ 35
Total Europe	974,273	1,018,365	+44,092
China	2,166	1,544	− 622
Japan	10,331	13,835	+ 3,504
India	190	216	+ 26
Turkey in Asia	6,157	6,354	+ 197
Other Asia	5,081	351	− 4,730
Total Asia	23,925	22,300	− 1,625
Africa	757	712	− 45
Australia, Tasmania, and New Zealand	2,091	1,682	− 409
Pacific islands, not specified	36	51	+ 15
British North America	2,168	5,063	+ 2,895
British Honduras	123	80	− 43
Other Central America	1,072	1,060	− 12
Mexico	2,637	1,997	− 640
South America	2,576	2,757	+ 181
West Indies	16,641	13,656	− 2,985
Other countries	200	33,012	+32,812
Grand total	1,026,499	1,100,735	+74,236

An encouraging feature of the year's immigration shown by Table III is the fact that while 913,955 of the admitted aliens ranged in age from 14 to 44 and 136,273 were less than 14 years of age, only 50,507 had reached or past the prime age of 45.

Of the aliens admitted during the year 265,068 could neither read nor write and 4,755 could read but not write. The corresponding figures for the year 1905 were 230,882 and 8,209, respectively. These figures for both years are exclusive of aliens aged less than 14 years. So that taking the 913,955 between the ages of 14 and 45 and the 50,507 aged 45 or over, a total of 964,462, who arrived in 1906, and comparing such number with 269,823, the total of those who could neither read nor write and those who could read but not write, we find that about 28 per cent of the said total number of aliens were illiterates. This is an increase of about 2 per cent over the percentage shown in 1905, viz, 26 per cent, which was an increase of 1 per cent over that of the preceding year.

As to the financial condition of those admitted, 698,401 had less than $50 each in their possession, while 112,679 possessed over that amount each. The man of mercenary mind who regards the accumulation of wealth, by the individual and the nation, as the thing most to be desired will note with satisfaction the total amount of money shown by the aliens admitted to the country during the year, $25,109,413. But if there could be set opposite that amount the sum of money sent out of the country during the year by the resident aliens of the laboring class, considerable in number, who transmit to the countries whence they came, and in which they still have family ties, all of their earnings except so much as is required for a bare sustenance here, doubtless that feeling of satisfaction would be modified. In 1905 the total amount shown by arriving aliens was $25,159,012—nearly $50,000 more than that shown by the considerably larger number of aliens arriving in 1906. It is extremely interesting to note the difference in financial condition between certain of the races. For instance, while the number of Hebrew aliens admitted was more than three times as great as the number of English, the former brought $2,362,125 with them, and the latter $2,610,439; while the 144,954 Germans and Scandinavians brought $5,091,594, the 263,655 South Italians and Greeks brought only $4,183,398; and while 16,463 Scotch were able to show $820,759, more than twice as many members of the Slovak race produced only $526,028.

During the year 12,432 aliens were debarred. It is instructive to observe the details of this subject furnished by Table III, especially if a comparison is made between the figures therein given as to the principal causes of rejection and similar items contained in the reports for 1904 and 1905, respectively. For this purpose the following comparative statement is inserted:

Cause of rejection.	1904.	1905.	1906.	Cause of rejection.	1904.	1905.	1906.
Idiocy	16	38	92	Conviction of crime	35	39	205
Insanity	33	92	139	Imported for prostitution	9	24	30
Pauperism	4,708	7,898	7,069	Contract laborers	1,501	1,164	2,314
Contagious diseases	1,560	2,198	2,273				

The constant increase in the number of aliens afflicted with contagious diseases, insanity, and idiocy is significant. That subject is fully discussed under subtitle 3 of this report (p. 61), and needs only passing notice here. Attention is also called to the fact that the number of contract laborers apprehended and turned back during the past year is almost double the number so debarred in 1905.

Another interesting feature of Table III is the column showing, by races, the number of aliens who have been afforded aid in hospitals of this country—a total of 9,300, of whom 2,495 belonged to the Hebrew race, 2,121 to the Italian, 1,000 to the Polish, and 867 to the German, the balance being divided between the other races in numbers ranging from 424 down to 1.

The three columns under the heading "Returned" in Table III show that in the cases of 676 aliens warrants of deportation have been executed, after granting a hearing in which to show cause, if any, why expulsion should not be effected. This has been accomplished solely by administrative officers, without any cause for complaint, and at a relatively small cost to the Government. During the last six months of the year detailed figures were kept concerning the races to which aliens ordered deported belonged, and the specific causes leading to the order for their expulsion, which details are shown by Table III A.

TABLE III.—IMMIGRANT ALIENS ADMITTED AND ALIENS DEPORTED, BY RACE OR PEOPLE, DURING THE YEAR ENDED JUNE 30, 1906.

ADMITTED.

Race or people.	Males.	Females.	Total.	Under 14 years.	14 to 44 years.	45 years and over.	Illiteracy, 14 years and over.		Aliens bringing—		Total amount of money shown.	Have been in the United States before.
							Can read, but can not write.	Can neither read nor write.	$50 or over.	Less than $50.		
African (black)	2,355	1,431	3,786	346	3,286	154	21	401	501	2,373	$93,423	963
Armenian	1,423	472	1,895	223	1,598	74	2	458	167	1,220	68,280	185
Bohemian and Moravian	7,418	5,540	12,958	2,678	9,578	702	8	172	1,415	7,067	377,057	450
Bulgarian, Servian, Montenegrin	11,104	444	11,548	224	11,104	220	9	4,726	267	10,422	197,540	405
Chinese	1,397	88	1,485	67	1,210	208	1	79	225	1,133	29,768	899
Croatian and Slovenian	38,287	5,985	44,272	1,674	41,653	945	76	16,941	964	38,313	582,503	5,595
Cuban	3,769	1,822	5,591	963	4,090	538	7	209	1,876	1,761	186,289	3,100
Dalmatian, Bosnian, Herzegovinian	4,346	222	4,568	77	4,398	93	8	1,980	231	4,107	86,724	216
Dutch and Flemish	6,526	3,209	9,735	1,706	7,442	587	6	316	2,357	3,682	458,773	1,320
East Indian	252	19	271	15	245	11	1	77	111	75	17,016	25
English	28,010	17,069	45,079	6,081	33,935	5,063	70	305	19,752	13,677	2,610,439	12,345
Finnish	9,525	4,611	14,136	1,005	12,840	291	81	121	925	11,284	293,825	1,958
French	5,924	4,455	10,379	889	8,482	1,008	11	207	4,951	3,118	753,025	3,483
German	51,427	35,386	86,813	13,076	68,282	5,455	166	3,645	18,116	42,536	3,549,465	11,477
Greek	22,266	861	23,127	718	22,174	235	12	5,256	1,571	20,013	545,611	1,303
Hebrew	80,086	73,662	153,748	43,620	101,875	8,253	292	29,444	8,151	50,720	2,362,125	2,666
Irish	20,846	20,113	40,959	1,868	37,232	1,859	66	823	5,745	27,595	1,082,332	8,785
Italian (north)	36,542	9,744	46,286	3,993	40,684	1,609	44	5,042	5,127	33,437	1,237,404	6,674
Italian (south)	190,992	49,536	240,528	26,546	202,888	11,094	78	114,957	11,267	179,867	3,637,787	31,430
Japanese	12,756	1,487	14,243	146	13,821	276	1	6,016	4,114	9,083	442,909	1,531
Korean	103	24	127	21	103	3		37	15	24	2,044	8
Lithuanian	9,429	4,828	14,257	1,270	12,765	222	1,041	6,934	379	10,970	165,558	401
Magyar	31,760	12,501	44,261	3,974	38,746	1,541	29	5,074	1,521	30,647	621,077	4,343
Mexican	93	48	141	21	105	15		1	78	19	10,718	79
Pacific Islander	10	3	13	1	10	2		6	3	1	588	1
Polish	66,410	29,425	95,835	8,941	84,860	2,034	2,308	29,927	1,945	74,136	1,103,955	5,737
Portuguese	5,096	3,633	8,729	1,821	6,171	737	15	4,667	598	4,897	129,991	1,190
Roumanian	10,561	864	11,425	201	10,769	455	13	4,059	167	10,615	174,096	525
Russian	4,750	1,064	5,814	580	5,047	187	37	2,003	613	3,656	156,251	266
Ruthenian (Russniak)	12,310	3,947	16,257	592	15,262	403	76	8,743	162	14,810	182,164	1,584
Scandinavian	36,092	22,049	58,141	5,290	50,214	2,637	112	154	6,394	40,623	1,542,129	9,729
Scotch	10,883	5,580	16,463	2,117	12,978	1,368	9	52	6,367	6,191	820,759	3,353
Slovak	26,605	11,616	38,221	3,415	33,796	1,010	105	7,544	662	30,752	526,028	7,084

Spanish	4,460	872	5,332	378	4,509	445	22	421	2,131	2,278	343,938	1,975
Spanish-American	1,105	480	1,585	270	1,179	136	4	24	1,051	154	151,977	597
Syrian	4,100	1,724	5,824	886	4,712	226	9	2,698	999	3,193	236,473	753
Turkish	1,946	87	2,033	38	1,952	43	4	1,139	193	1,738	74,774	159
Welsh	1,660	707	2,367	297	1,851	219	7	23	851	859	145,281	480
West Indian (except Cuban)	869	607	1,476	218	1,123	135	3	23	596	564	76,779	481
Other peoples	970	57	1,027	27	986	14	1	364	121	791	32,568	69
Total	764,463	336,272	1,100,735	136,273	913,955	50,507	4,755	265,068	112,679	698,401	25,109,413	133,624

[Table continued on page 10.]

TABLE III.—IMMIGRANT ALIENS ADMITTED AND ALIENS DEPORTED, BY RACE OR PEOPLE, DURING THE YEAR ENDED JUNE 30, 1906—Cont'd.

DEBARRED, RETURNED, AND RELIEVED IN HOSPITAL.

Race or people.	Debarred.													Returned.			Relieved in hospital.
	Idiots.	Insane persons.[a]	Paupers, or likely to become public charges.[b]	Loathsome or dangerous contagious diseases.	Convicts.	Polygamists.	Anarchists.	Prostitutes.	Persons who procure or attempt to bring in prostitutes.	Under sec. 11, act of 1903.	Contract laborers.[c]	Under Chinese exclusion act.	Total debarred.	Within 1 year for causes arising subsequent to landing.	Within 3 years, because here in violation of law.	Total returned.	
African (black)		1	36	10	1			3		1	18		70	2	5	7	5
Armenian			26	34							4		64				37
Bohemian and Moravian	5	2	67	14						7	1		96		8	8	99
Bulgarian, Servian, Montenegrin			126	12							633		771	1	6	7	50
Chinese			1	84								122	207				
Croatian and Slovenian	2	1	202	76	2						166		449		6	6	212
Cuban			26	8			1	1	1		5		42				2
Dalmatian, Bosnian, Herzegovinian			39	8							124		171	1	1	2	29
Dutch and Flemish	1		36	3				1		1	17		59		8	8	55
East Indian	2		10	6						1	5		24		2	2	2
English	4	15	404	18	1	1		1		2	82		528	3	36	39	118
Finnish	1	2	55	35						1	15		109	1	11	12	56
French		8	67	9	1			15		1	15		116		23	23	38
German	9	14	359	88	3			2		11	32		518	9	91	100	867
Greek		4	365	31	1					24	432		857		10	10	189
Hebrew	23	23	1,131	275						38	33		1,523	5	76	81	2,495
Irish	2	24	149	11	1					4	14		205	3	61	64	214
Italian (north)	5		127	32	6			3		2	18		193		13	13	345
Italian (south)	29	19	2,107	317	182			1		60	265		2,980	4	60	64	1,776
Japanese			84	266				1	1		18		370		11	11	1
Korean			3	8							1		12		2	2	
Lithuanian			52	103						1	7		163		4	4	228
Magyar	1	2	129	73	1					3	22		231	1	46	47	424
Mexican			11	2									13	2		2	1
Pacific Islander															1	1	
Polish	3	7	385	160	3					7	57		622	8	46	54	1,000
Portuguese	2	1	83	9						3	11		109	1		1	43
Roumanian		1	71	23							82		177		2	2	30
Russian			31	26							9		66		2	2	28

Ruthenian (Russniak)			118	12	2			1		2	17		152		6	6	103
Scandinavian		5	142	50						2	19		218	8	35	43	179
Scotch		5	142	11						2	17		177	8	5	13	47
Slovak	2	2	153	37	1					3	12		210	4	9	13	325
Spanish	1		33	17				1			38		90		3	3	33
Spanish-American			4	5									9		1	1	7
Syrian			196	358		3				4	33		594		9	9	184
Turkish			47	24		1					10		82		1	1	11
Welsh		1	12								2		15		1	1	8
West Indian (except Cuban)		1	11	6									18		4	4	26
Other peoples		1	29	12							80		122		10	10	33
Total	92	139	7,069	2,273	205	5	1	30	2	180	2,314	122	12,432	61	615	676	9,300

[a] Includes those who have been insane within five years, those who have had two attacks of insanity, and epileptics.
[b] Includes professional beggars.
[c] Includes those who have been deported as contract laborers within one year.

TABLE III A.—ALIENS WITHIN THE UNITED STATES ORDERED

Race or people.	Deportation of aliens in these										
	Anarchists prior to admission.	Contract laborers and aliens admitted within one year subsequent to their deportation as such.	Convicts prior to admission.	Epileptics prior to admission.	Idiots prior to admission.	Insane at the time of admission.	Insane within five years prior to admission.	Insanity; two attacks prior to admission.	Afflicted with a loathsome or a dangerous contagious disease at the time of admission.	Prostitutes prior to admission and women imported for purposes of prostitution.	Procurers of or persons attempting to bring in prostitutes or women for purposes of prostitution.
African (black)	0	0	0	0	0	0	0	0	0	0	0
Armenian	0	0	0	0	0	0	0	0	0	0	0
Bohemian and Moravian	0	0	0	0	0	0	0	0	0	0	0
Bulgarian, Servian, and Montenegrin	0	0	1	0	0	0	0	0	0	0	0
Chinese	0	0	0	0	0	0	0	0	0	0	0
Croatian and Slovenian	0	0	0	0	0	0	0	0	1	0	0
Cuban	0	0	1	0	0	0	0	0	0	1	0
Dalmatian, Bosnian, and Herzegovinian	0	0	0	0	0	0	0	0	0	0	0
Dutch and Flemish	0	0	0	0	0	0	0	0	0	0	0
East Indian	0	0	0	0	0	0	0	0	0	0	0
English	0	9	0	1	0	0	1	0	1	0	0
Finnish	0	0	0	0	0	0	0	0	0	0	0
French	0	5	1	0	0	0	1	0	0	6	0
German	0	0	0	0	1	1	0	0	0	0	0
Greek	0	0	1	0	0	0	1	0	0	0	0
Hebrew	0	0	0	0	0	0	0	0	0	0	0
Irish	0	0	0	1	0	0	2	0	0	0	0
Italian (north)	0	0	1	0	0	0	0	0	0	0	0
Italian (south)	0	0	1	1	0	1	0	0	0	2	0
Japanese	0	0	0	0	0	0	0	0	0	3	0
Korean	0	0	0	0	0	0	0	0	0	0	0
Lithuanian	0	0	0	0	0	0	0	0	0	0	0
Magyar	0	1	0	0	0	0	0	0	0	0	0
Mexican	0	3	0	0	0	0	0	0	0	5	0
Pacific Islander	0	0	0	0	0	0	0	0	0	0	0
Polish	0	0	1	0	0	0	1	0	0	0	0
Portuguese	0	0	0	0	0	0	0	0	0	0	0
Roumanian	0	0	0	0	0	0	0	0	0	0	0
Russian	0	0	0	0	0	1	0	0	0	0	0
Ruthenian (Russniak)	0	0	0	0	0	0	0	0	0	0	0
Scandinavian	0	0	0	0	0	0	1	0	0	0	0
Scotch	0	0	0	0	0	0	0	0	0	0	0
Slovak	0	0	0	0	0	0	1	0	0	0	0
Spanish	0	1	0	0	0	0	0	0	0	0	0
Spanish-American	0	0	0	0	0	0	0	0	0	0	0
Syrian	0	0	0	0	0	0	0	0	0	0	0
Turkish	0	0	0	0	0	0	0	0	0	0	0
Welsh	0	0	0	0	0	0	0	0	0	0	0
West Indian (except Cuban)	0	0	0	0	0	0	0	0	0	0	0
All other peoples	0	0	0	0	0	0	0	0	0	0	0
Total (by class)	0	19	7	3	1	3	8	0	2	17	0

DEPORTED DURING SIX MONTHS ENDED JUNE 30, 1906.

classes is mandatory—act of 1903.											Deportation only with alien's consent—Rule 17. (Public charges from causes arising subsequent to admission, showing mental or physical affliction.)				
				Public charges from causes existing prior to admission (showing mental or physical affliction, if any).											
Professional beggars and paupers prior to admission.	Polygamists prior to admission.	Entered surreptitiously or without due process of law.	Total.	Insanity.	Other mental afflictions.	Loathsome or dangerous contagious disease.	Dependent members of family.	All others.	Total.	Total.	Insanity.	Loathsome or dangerous contagious disease.	All others.	Total.	Total (by race).
0	0	0	0	1	0	0	0	1	2	2	0	0	0	0	2
0	0	0	0	0	0	0	0	0	0	0	0	0	0	0	0
0	0	0	0	3	0	0	1	0	4	4	0	0	0	0	4
0	0	0	1	1	0	0	0	0	1	2	0	0	0	0	2
0	0	0	0	0	0	0	0	0	0	0	0	0	0	0	0
0	0	2	3	0	1	3	0	3	7	10	0	0	0	0	10
0	0	0	2	0	0	0	0	0	0	2	0	0	0	0	2
0	0	0	0	0	0	0	0	0	0	0	0	0	0	0	0
0	0	0	0	0	0	1	0	0	1	1	0	0	0	0	1
0	0	2	2	0	0	0	0	0	0	2	0	0	0	0	2
0	0	6	18	11	2	2	6	1	22	40	0	1	1	2	42
0	0	0	0	4	0	0	0	3	7	7	0	0	0	0	7
0	0	7	20	6	0	0	0	0	6	26	0	0	0	0	26
0	0	5	7	19	0	1	2	5	27	34	0	1	0	1	35
0	0	1	3	1	0	1	0	2	4	7	0	0	0	0	7
0	0	1	1	39	2	5	0	2	48	49	0	1	3	4	53
0	0	2	5	21	0	3	0	7	31	36	0	0	1	1	37
0	0	0	1	2	0	0	1	1	4	5	0	1	0	1	6
0	0	5	10	7	1	7	0	8	23	33	1	1	0	2	35
0	0	13	16	0	0	0	0	0	0	16	0	0	0	0	16
0	0	1	1	0	0	0	0	0	0	1	0	0	0	0	1
0	0	0	0	0	0	0	0	0	0	0	0	0	0	0	0
0	0	1	2	6	2	1	0	2	11	13	0	1	2	3	16
0	0	59	67	1	0	0	0	2	3	70	0	0	0	0	70
0	0	0	0	0	0	0	0	0	0	0	0	0	0	0	0
0	0	0	2	11	2	3	5	6	27	29	0	0	3	3	32
0	0	0	0	3	0	0	0	0	3	3	0	0	0	0	3
0	0	0	0	1	0	0	0	0	1	1	0	0	0	0	1
0	0	0	0	0	1	0	0	0	1	1	0	0	0	0	1
0	0	0	0	1	0	0	0	4	5	5	1	0	0	1	6
0	0	0	2	14	3	0	1	5	23	25	0	0	0	0	25
0	0	1	1	0	0	1	0	0	1	2	0	0	0	0	2
0	0	0	1	3	0	0	3	1	7	8	0	0	0	0	8
0	0	1	2	0	0	0	0	0	0	2	0	0	0	0	2
0	0	0	0	0	0	0	0	0	0	0	0	0	0	0	0
0	0	6	6	1	0	0	0	1	2	7	0	0	0	0	8
0	0	0	0	0	0	0	0	1	1	1	0	0	0	0	1
0	0	0	0	1	0	0	0	0	1	1	0	0	0	0	1
0	0	0	0	0	0	0	0	0	0	0	0	0	0	0	0
0	0	0	0	0	0	0	0	0	0	0	0	0	0	0	0
0	0	113	173	157	14	28	19	55	273	446	2	6	10	18	464

Chart 1 is inserted at this point, as it bears upon part of the data furnished by Table III. Said chart shows the proportion of aliens refused admission, and the proportion of those admitted that afterwards became public charges and were returned under the provisions of the immigration laws to the countries whence they came. It is interesting to note the balance between the debarred and the returned, as shown by the uniformity of divergence and convergence of the wave lines representing these two classes.

During the fifteen years shown about 72,000 aliens have been debarred, of which number 66 per cent were paupers or aliens likely to become public charges, 17 per cent were contract laborers, and 13 per cent were aliens suffering from loathsome or dangerous contagious diseases.

Table III B is a repetition of the statement of rejections since 1891, which was first published in the report for 1904, and which was inserted, without numerical designation, on page 10 of last year's report. The figures for the year just past have been added thereto.

TABLE III B.—ALIENS REFUSED ADMISSION AT SEAPORTS AND THOSE RETURNED AFTER LANDING DURING THE FIFTEEN YEARS 1892 TO 1906, INCLUSIVE.

Year.	Immigrants.	Debarred.														Returned in 1 year after landing.	Returned in 3 years after landing.
		Idiots.	Insane persons.	Paupers, or likely to become public charges.	Loathsome or dangerous contagious diseases.	Convicts.	Polygamists.	Anarchists.	Prostitutes.	Persons who procure or attempt to bring in prostitutes.	Assisted immigrants.	Accompanying aliens.	Contract laborers.	Under provisions of Chinese exclusion act.	Total debarred.		
1892	579,663	4	17	1,002	80	26	...	...	80	...	23	...	932	...	2,164	637	...
1893	439,730	3	8	431	81	12	...	...	...	...	...	...	518	...	1,053	577	...
1894	285,631	4	5	802	15	8	...	...	2	...	...	...	553	...	1,389	417	...
1895	258,536	6	...	1,714	...	4	...	...	...	...	1	...	694	...	2,419	177	...
1896	343,267	1	10	2,010	2	...	...	...	...	...	...	...	776	...	2,799	238	...
1897	230,832	1	6	1,277	1	1	...	...	...	...	3	...	328	...	1,617	263	...
1898	229,299	1	12	2,261	258	2	...	...	...	...	79	...	417	...	3,030	199	...
1899	311,715	1	19	2,590	348	8	...	...	...	...	82	...	741	...	3,798	263	...
1900	448,572	1	32	2,974	393	4	...	...	7	...	2	...	833	...	4,246	356	...
1901	487,918	6	16	2,798	309	7	...	...	3	...	50	...	327	...	3,516	363	...
1902	648,743	7	27	3,944	709	9	...	...	3	...	...	...	275	...	4,974	465	...
1903	857,046	1	23	5,812	1,773	51	1	...	13	...	9	...	1,086	...	8,769	547	...
1904	812,870	16	33	4,798	1,560	35	...	1	9	3	38	...	1,501	...	7,994	300	479
1905	1,026,499	38	92	7,898	2,198	39	3	1	24	4	19	...	1,164	...	11,879	98	747
1906	1,100,735	92	139	7,069	2,273	205	5	1	30	2	...	180	2,314	122	12,432	61	615

Table III C (numbered III A in the report for 1905) is designed to show by ports and causes the number of citizens of Canada and Mexico who have during the year been refused admission—a total of 2,865. The point of chief interest is the striking contrast between the figures for the two countries, it having been necessary to turn back on the Canadian border only 486 Canadians, while on the Mexican border 2,366 Mexicans were refused admission. The remaining 13 shown by the table are miscellaneous cases arising at several of the seaports. The contrast prevails throughout the list of causes, 1,588 paupers having been rejected on the Mexican as against 331 on the Canadian border, and 331 diseased, 327 contract laborers, and 83 prostitutes on the former as against 18, 104, and 18, respectively, on the latter.

CHART I

FOR FURTHER INFORMATION SEE PAGE 14

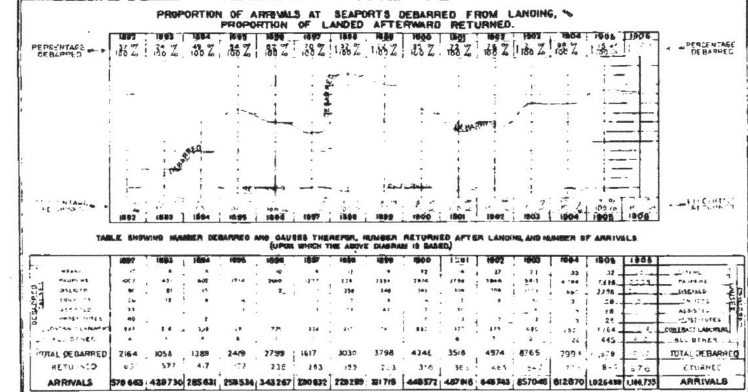

TABLE SHOWING NUMBER DEBARRED AND CAUSES THEREFOR, NUMBER RETURNED AFTER LANDING, AND NUMBER OF ARRIVALS. (UPON WHICH THE ABOVE DIAGRAM IS BASED)

	1892	1893	1894	1895	1896	1897	1898	1899	1900	1901	1902	1903	1904	1905	1906	
DEBARRED CAUSES: INSANE	[illegible]	6	5		10	6	12	[illegible]	32	[illegible]	17	[illegible]	33	32	[illegible]	INSANE
PAUPERS	[illegible]	[illegible]	[illegible]	[illegible]	[illegible]	[illegible]	[illegible]	[illegible]	[illegible]	[illegible]	[illegible]	[illegible]	[illegible]	[illegible]	[illegible]	PAUPERS
DISEASED	[illegible]	81	15		2		[illegible]	[illegible]	[illegible]	[illegible]	[illegible]	[illegible]	[illegible]	[illegible]	[illegible]	DISEASED
CONVICTS	[illegible]	12	8	4		[illegible]	[illegible]	8	[illegible]	3	9	[illegible]	3	[illegible]	[illegible]	CONVICTS
ASSISTED	[illegible]			1		1	[illegible]	[illegible]	[illegible]	[illegible]		[illegible]	[illegible]	[illegible]	[illegible]	ASSISTED
PROSTITUTES	[illegible]		2						[illegible]	[illegible]	[illegible]	[illegible]	[illegible]	[illegible]	[illegible]	PROSTITUTES
CONTRACT LABORERS	[illegible]	[illegible]	[illegible]	[illegible]	[illegible]	[illegible]	[illegible]	[illegible]	[illegible]	[illegible]	[illegible]	[illegible]	[illegible]	[illegible]	[illegible]	CONTRACT LABORERS
ALL OTHER	4	[illegible]	4	6	1					6	7	2	26	445	[illegible]	ALL OTHER
TOTAL DEBARRED	2164	1058	1389	2419	2799	1617	3030	3798	4246	3516	4974	8765	7994	[illegible]	[illegible]	TOTAL DEBARRED
RETURNED	[illegible]	577	[illegible]	177	238	263	[illegible]	[illegible]	[illegible]	[illegible]	[illegible]	[illegible]	[illegible]	[illegible]	[illegible]	RETURNED
ARRIVALS	579663	439730	285631	258536	343267	230832	229299	311715	448572	487918	648743	857046	812870	1026499	1,100,735	ARRIVALS

TABLE III C.—CITIZENS OF FOREIGN CONTIGUOUS COUNTRIES REFUSED ADMISSION TO THE UNITED STATES DURING THE FISCAL YEAR ENDED JUNE 30, 1906.

Station.	Idiots.	Insane persons.[a]	Paupers, or likely to become public charges.[b]	Loathsome or dangerous contagious diseases.	Convicts.	Prostitutes.	Persons who procure or attempt to bring in prostitutes.	Accompanying aliens.	Contract laborers.[c]	Total debarred.
CANADIAN BORDER STATIONS.										
Alburg, Vt.			1							1
Black Rock, N. Y.			28	2		1			5	36
Blaine, Wash.		2	7			2				11
Brockville, Ontario			7							7
Calais, Me.			9		1					10
Cape Vincent, N. Y.			3			1			1	5
Charlotte, N. Y.			3							3
Clayton, N. Y.			1			1				2
Cornwall, Ontario			7						1	8
Detroit, Mich.		1	30	4		6		1	14	56
Fort Covington, N. Y.									1	1
Halifax, Nova Scotia			4	1	1	2				8
Houlton, Me.			39							39
Montreal, Canada			33						27	60
Morristown, N. Y.			10		2					12
Neche, N. Dak.				1						1
Newport, Vt.			6							6
Niagara Falls, N. Y.			19	1					23	43
Northport, Wash.			2							2
North Stratford, N. H.			31							31
Ogdensburg, N. Y.			18	1					8	27
Oswego, N. Y.			2			5				7
Pembina, N. Dak.			1						2	3
Portal, N. Dak.									3	3
Port Huron, Mich.		3	34		2				12	51
Rainy River, Ontario			3							3
St. Johns, New Brunswick			8	2					3	13
Sault Ste. Marie, Mich.			8	1						9
Sumas, Wash.			1	1					1	3
Swanton, Vt.			2							2
Sweet Grass, Mont.			1							1
Vanceboro, Me.			3	1					1	5
Victoria, B. C.			5						1	6
Winnipeg, Manitoba			5	3					1	9
Yarmouth, Nova Scotia					2					2
Total		6	331	18	8	18		1	104	486
MEXICAN BORDER STATIONS.										
Brownsville, Tex.			157	4	1	27	2		63	254
Eagle Pass, Tex.	3	2	226	4		3		2	77	317
El Paso, Tex.	1	6	524	288	1	28		15	57	920
Laredo, Tex.	1	3	529	15		11			127	686
Douglas, Ariz.			25			5				30
Naco, Ariz.			62	20						82
Nogales, Ariz.			65			9			3	77
Total	5	11	1,588	331	2	83	2	17	327	2,366
SEAPORT STATIONS.										
Boston, Mass.		1								1
New York, N. Y.	1			1				1		3
San Diego, Cal.				3						3
San Francisco, Cal.				6						6
Total	1	1		10				1		13
Grand total	6	18	1,919	359	10	101	2	19	431	2,865

[a] Includes those who have been insane within five years; those who have had two attacks of insanity, and epileptics.
[b] Includes professional beggars.
[c] Includes those who have been deported as contract laborers within one year.

Table IV furnishes a convenient means of comparing the number of aliens, male and female, admitted during each month of the fiscal year 1906 with the number for each month of the preceding year. Comparisons with previous years can readily be made by referring to former reports.

TABLE IV.—IMMIGRANT ALIENS ADMITTED INTO THE UNITED STATES, BY MONTHS, DURING THE FISCAL YEARS ENDED JUNE 30, 1905 AND 1906.

Month.	1905.			1906.		
	Males.	Females.	Total.	Males.	Females.	Total.
July	37,008	20,783	57,791	49,227	26,863	76,090
August	36,645	23,132	59,777	38,896	24,513	63,409
September	39,204	33,562	72,766	45,265	32,284	77,549
October	42,452	32,873	75,325	52,409	34,349	86,758
November	46,630	24,407	71,037	38,787	22,587	61,374
December	44,369	18,288	62,657	41,159	20,957	62,116
January	42,527	13,709	56,236	36,034	15,093	51,127
February	52,528	14,577	67,105	52,507	16,189	68,696
March	101,756	25,152	126,908	104,922	27,470	132,392
April	107,036	30,014	137,050	114,702	35,695	150,397
May	95,432	32,079	127,511	108,812	42,115	150,927
June	79,327	33,009	112,336	81,743	38,157	119,900
Total	724,914	301,585	1,026,499	764,463	336,272	1,100,735

Tables V to IX, inclusive, inserted hereinafter, while pregnant with information of interest and value, require no comment further than to repeat the injunction, contained in the last annual report of the Bureau, that neither the information in respect to the occupations nor that giving destinations is absolutely conclusive of the facts asserted, the stated occupations being those followed by the aliens before emigrating and possibly abandoned after landing in this country, and the stated destinations being those given by the aliens upon arrival, and, even if true, subject to change.

TABLE V.—IMMIGRANT ALIENS ADMITTED INTO THE UNITED STATES DURING THE FISCAL YEAR ENDED JUNE 30, 1906, SHOWING THE COUNTRIES OF LAST PERMANENT RESIDENCE AND THE RACES OR PEOPLES TO WHICH THEY BELONG.

Country of last permanent residence.	African (black).	Armenian.	Bohemian and Moravian (Czech).	Bulgarian, Servian, and Montenegrin.	Chinese.	Croatian and Slovenian.	Cuban.	Dalmatian, Bosnian, and Herzegovinian.	Dutch and Flemish.	East Indian.	English.	Finnish.	French.	German.	Greek.	Hebrew.	Irish.	Italian (north).	Italian (south).	Japanese.	Korean.
Austria-Hungary	1	1	12,635	3,224		43,157		4,424	61		10		42	34,848	9	14,884	2	1,914	48		
Belgium		1	1	16		6		1	3,958		20	6	851	103	9	59	4	7	8	1	
Bulgaria, Servia, and Montenegro		6		4,473		56		12					1	8	10	20		2			
Denmark						2			4		2	7	2	22		18					
France, including Corsica	6	16	7	5		7	6	1	127	1	216	4	6,957	504	173	479	40	335	64	11	1
German Empire	1		66	3		32			37		37	4	70	31,855	5	979	1	56	21	1	
Greece		3				3					4		2	6	19,398	23		1	6		
Italy, including Sicily and Sardinia	2	4	1	2		6	1		1		25		33	36	23	7	11	40,940	231,921		
Netherlands			3					1	4,767	1	15	1	9	68		51		2			
Norway			1								17	6		9		2		1			
Portugal, including Cape Verde and Azore islands	301								1		2				1	3		1	1		
Roumania		13		15		3							1	225	14	3,872		3	1		
Russian Empire		130	43	10	2	19			4		9	13,461	7	10,279	15	125,234	6	1	1		
Spain, including Canary and Balearic islands	3			1			9				7		17	6	2	5	1	9	9		
Sweden		1		1								28	2	20		38	1	5		1	
Switzerland						1			30		8		467	2,991		67	3	261	4		
Turkey in Europe	1	102		3,647		5		18			3		2	19	2,766	252		2			
United Kingdom	27	52	25	9	10	14	2	3	222	46	38,111	61	270	802	103	6,113	36,953	312	181	34	1
Other Europe											3		1	23	6	1		3	7		
Total Europe	342	329	12,782	11,406	12	43,311	18	4,460	9,212	48	38,489	13,578	8,734	81,874	22,534	152,107	37,022	43,855	232,272	48	2
China			1		1,296		1		4	29	69	1	12	47	7	3	6	4	1	5	6
Japan					2				4	2	46		2	22	2	7	2		3	13,710	1
India		1							1	155	34		1	11		1	5				
Turkey in Asia	1	1,420		16							2		4	4	106	209		4	1		
Other Asia		2		2					1	21	3		1	3	3	8			3	1	112
Total Asia	1	1,423	1	18	1,298		1		10	207	154	1	20	87	118	228	13	8	8	13,716	119

TABLE V.—IMMIGRANT ALIENS ADMITTED INTO THE UNITED STATES DURING THE FISCAL YEAR ENDED JUNE 30, 1906, SHOWING THE COUNTRIES OF LAST PERMANENT RESIDENCE AND THE RACES OR PEOPLES TO WHICH THEY BELONG—Continued.

Country of last permanent residence.	African (black).	Armenian.	Bohemian and Moravian (Czech).	Bulgarian, Servian, and Montenegrin.	Chinese.	Croatian and Slovenian.	Cuban.	Dalmatian, Bosnian, and Herzegovinian.	Dutch and Flemish.	East Indian.	English.	Finnish.	French.	German.	Greek.	Hebrew.	Irish.	Italian (north).	Italian (south).	Japanese.	Korean.
Africa	15	29	......	1	......	2	......	......	7	....	97	3	12	29	55	278	11	20	8	2	....
Australia, Tasmania, and New Zealand	3	......	5	1	......	13	......	33	1	....	1,087	8	9	101	16	20	155	5	10	1	....
Pacific islands, not specified	1	......	......	......	......	......	......	......	1	1	4	......	5	4	......	......	......	......	2	6	....
British North America	9	35	29	23	16	96	......	17	34	6	1,191	97	80	290	56	429	191	83	860	145	....
British Honduras	7	......	......	......	......	......	1	......	......	....	16	......	3	11	......	......	1	......	......	......	....
Other Central America	84	......	1	......	......	3	14	2	7	....	76	8	31	75	14	1	4	35	27	8	....
Mexico	4	......	11	5	7	8	13	9	19	2	261	10	149	287	10	6	22	128	45	231	3
South America	43	23	1	15	......	21	8	5	20	2	111	3	59	212	22	86	18	199	393	10	....
West Indies	3,018	1	7	1	7	4	4,448	1	74	1	1,334	13	164	125	44	34	25	66	79	5	1
United States	256	47	120	78	145	814	1,088	41	348	4	2,253	415	1,108	3,715	257	559	3,493	1,885	6,823	70	2
Other countries	3	8	1	......	......	......	......	......	2	....	6	......	5	3	1	......	4	2	1	1	....
Grand total	3,786	1,895	12,958	11,548	1,485	44,272	5,591	4,568	9,735	271	45,079	14,136	10,379	86,813	23,127	153,748	40,959	46,286	240,528	14,243	127

TABLE V.—IMMIGRANT ALIENS ADMITTED INTO THE UNITED STATES DURING THE FISCAL YEAR ENDED JUNE 30, 1906, SHOWING THE COUNTRIES OF LAST PERMANENT RESIDENCE AND THE RACES OR PEOPLES TO WHICH THEY BELONG—Continued.

Country of last permanent residence.	Lithuanian.	Magyar.	Mexican.	Pacific Islander.	Polish.	Portuguese.	Roumanian.	Russian.	Ruthenian (Russniak).	Scandinavian (Norwegians, Danes, and Swedes).	Scotch.	Slovak.	Spanish.	Spanish-American.	Syrian.	Turkish.	Welsh.	West Indian (other than Cuban).	Other peoples.	Grand total.
Austria-Hungary	38	42,848			43,803		10,811	67	15,689	50		36,550	5			14			3	265,138
Belgium		2			3		1			28	1		3	3		4	3			5,099
Bulgaria, Servia, and Montenegro		5			2		4					17				50				4,666
Denmark	3				35			3		7,643										7,741
France, including Corsica		21	13		23	3	18	60		43	6	3	73	45	81	20	1	12	4	9,386
German Empire	22	30	1		4,108		9	58	5	135	3	14	3	3		3	1		1	37,564
Greece															5	32			6	19,489
Italy, including Sicily and Sardinia		6	2		9	2	3	3		4	1	2	4	2	15	3			1	273,120
Netherlands		7			8			4		8									1	4,946
Norway										21,693	1									21,730
Portugal, including Cape Verde and Azore islands		2				8,198		1		2	1		3							8,517
Roumania	2	5			4		297	3	1			2	2			8			5	4,476
Russian Empire	13,697	10			46,204		10	5,282	259	937		4			18	3			20	215,665
Spain, including Canary and Balearic islands			1			13	1				1		1,701	47	3	1		19	65	1,921
Sweden					5			3		23,203	2									23,310
Switzerland		1			3		1	4		1				4						3,846
Turkey in Europe		5					81	1			1	3	2		454	1,543			603	9,510
United Kingdom	382	46	1	1	259	25	12	93	1	359	15,048	7	233	24	85	37	2,168	26	35	102,193
Other Europe										4										48
Total Europe	14,144	42,988	18	1	94,466	8,241	11,248	5,582	15,955	54,110	15,065	36,602	2,029	128	661	1,718	2,173	57	744	1,018,365
China							4	11		16	17			1		2			1	1,544
Japan			1		9			3		13	4		1	1						13,835
India					1						4					1			1	216
Turkey in Asia								3			1		2	1	4,353	186			41	6,354
Other Asia								5		1	1				34	26			124	351
Total Asia			1		10		4	22		30	27		3	3	4,387	215			167	22,300

TABLE V.—IMMIGRANT ALIENS ADMITTED INTO THE UNITED STATES DURING THE FISCAL YEAR ENDED JUNE 30, 1906, SHOWING THE COUNTRIES OF LAST PERMANENT RESIDENCE AND THE RACES OR PEOPLES TO WHICH THEY BELONG—Continued.

Country of last permanent residence.	Lithuanian.	Magyar.	Mexican.	Pacific Islander.	Polish.	Portuguese.	Roumanian.	Russian.	Ruthenian (Russniak).	Scandinavian (Norwegians, Danes, and Swedes).	Scotch.	Slovak.	Spanish.	Spanish-American.	Syrian.	Turkish.	Welsh.	West Indian (other than Cuban).	Other peoples.	Grand total.
Africa	5	1			2	7	1	2		16	28		6	1	39	12	1		22	712
Australia, Tasmania, and New Zealand				1	1	1	3	3		46	141		1		8	2	6		1	1,682
Pacific islands, not specified				11	1			3		1	2		2	5	2					51
British North America	15	180			249	3	33	29	18	325	380	46	3	4	46	11	23	10	1	5,063
British Honduras			1			2					2			20		11		5		80
Other Central America		3	2		2	2		3		31	18		122	450	7	2	2	24	2	1,060
Mexico		5	82		4	1		22		60	21	3	315	44	175	20	1	2	12	1,997
South America	17	10	1		27	101	56	74		27	12	5	290	633	192	5		35	11	2,757
West Indies			30		3	153	12	14		113	46	1	2,080	248	175	21	6	1,300	2	13,656
United States	76	1,074	6		1,059	217	68	59	284	3,367	716	1,564	479	49	132	16	154	43	13	32,897
Other countries					1	1		1		15	5		2				1		52	115
Grand total	14,257	44,261	141	13	95,835	8,729	11,425	5,814	16,257	58,141	16,463	38,221	5,332	1,585	5,824	2,033	2,367	1,476	1,027	1,100,735

Chart 2 (numbered 3 in the report for 1905) shows approximately areas of racial grand divisions of Europe, together with number and ethnic character of aliens arriving from each European country. A comparison of the number of aliens of the different racial subdivisions and grand divisions for the fiscal year 1905 is also shown.

In preparing the said chart, as originally presented, most of the various subdivisions of races coming from Europe were, with the assistance of Prof. Otis T. Mason, of the National Museum, grouped into four grand divisions, as follows:

Teutonic division, from northern Europe: German, Scandinavian, English, Dutch, Flemish, and Finnish.

Iberic division, from southern Europe: South Italian, Greek, Portuguese, and Spanish; also Syrian from Turkey in Asia.

Keltic division, from western Europe: Irish, Welsh, Scotch, French, and North Italian.

Slavic division, from eastern Europe: Bohemian, Moravian, Bulgarian, Servian, Montenegrin, Croatian, Slovenian, Dalmatian, Bosnian, Herzegovinian, Hebrew, Lithuanian, Polish, Roumanian, Russian, Ruthenian, and Slovak.

The Mongolic division has also been added, to include Chinese, Japanese, Korean, East Indian, Pacific Islanders, and Filipino.

Under "All others" have been included Magyar, Turkish, Armenian, African (black), and subdivisions native to the Western Hemisphere.

By reason of blood mixture this classification is somewhat arbitrary, especially with regard to Finnish, Scotch, and southern Germans.

With regard to grand divisions of race, during the past year 37 per cent of the entire immigration, or 408,903 aliens, were Slavic; 28 per cent, or 283,540, were Iberic; 19 per cent, or 213,904, were Teutonic, and 11 per cent, or 116,454, were Keltic. There was an increase in the proportion of Iberic from 21 per cent in 1905 to 28 per cent in 1906, while the Teutonic and Keltic decreased from 22 and 12 per cent, respectively, in 1905 to 19 and 11 per cent in 1906. The Slavic remained the same.

TABLE VI.—IMMIGRANT ALIENS ADMITTED INTO THE UNITED STATES, BY COUNTRIES, DURING THE FISCAL YEAR ENDED JUNE 30, 1906.

Country of last permanent residence.	Males.	Females.	Total.
Austria	75,975	35,623	111,598
Hungary	113,469	40,071	153,540
Belgium	3,520	1,579	5,099
Bulgaria, Servia, and Montenegro	4,561	105	4,666
Denmark	5,068	2,673	7,741
France, including Corsica	5,591	3,795	9,386
German Empire	21,747	15,817	37,564
Greece	18,563	926	19,489
Italy, including Sicily and Sardinia	216,115	57,005	273,120
Netherlands	3,042	1,904	4,946
Norway	14,131	7,599	21,730
Portugal, including Cape Verde and Azore islands	5,012	3,505	8,517
Roumania	2,298	2,178	4,476
Russian Empire, and Finland	127,253	88,412	215,665
Spain, including Canary and Balearic islands	1,571	350	1,921
Sweden	13,835	9,475	23,310
Switzerland	2,460	1,386	3,846
Turkey in Europe	9,130	380	9,510
United Kingdom:			
England	30,983	18,508	49,491
Ireland	18,234	16,761	34,995
Scotland	10,500	5,366	15,866
Wales	1,305	536	1,841
Other Europe	35	13	48
Total Europe	704,398	313,967	1,018,365
China	1,404	140	1,544
Japan	12,344	1,491	13,835
India	187	29	216
Turkey in Asia	4,538	1,816	6,354
Other Asia	306	45	351
Total Asia	18,779	3,521	22,300
Africa	562	150	712
Australia, Tasmania, and New Zealand	1,165	517	1,682
Pacific Islands, not specified	36	15	51
British North America	4,386	677	5,063
British Honduras	43	37	80
Other Central America	795	265	1,060
Mexico	1,643	354	1,997
South America	1,942	815	2,757
West Indies	11,101	2,555	13,656
United States	19,521	13,376	32,897
All other countries	92	23	115
Grand total	764,463	336,272	1,100,735

TABLE VII.—IMMIGRANT ALIENS ADMITTED INTO THE UNITED STATES DURING THE FISCAL YEAR ENDED JUNE 30, 1906, SHOWING DESTINATIONS BY RACES OR PEOPLES.

State.	African (black).	Armenian.	Bohemian and Moravian (Czech).	Bulgarian, Servian, and Montenegrin.	Chinese.	Croatian and Slovenian.	Cuban.	Dalmatian, Bosnian, and Herzegovinian.	Dutch and Flemish.	East Indian.	English.	Finnish.	French.	German.	Greek.	Hebrew.	Irish.	Italian (north).	Italian (south).	Japanese.	Korean.
Alabama	31			92		53	48	1	23		93	1	12	82	57	152	15	39	386	1	
Alaska			1	22		4		8			16	21	9	6		1	1	3	2	14	
Arizona			5	61	5	67		61	5		271	10	15	30	3	12	23	250	25	25	
Arkansas	2		10			45			6		31		4	109	15	32	8	88	12		
California	23	43	44	68	910	344	12	387	120	25	1,981	249	1,053	1,404	328	300	812	4,875	1,000	2,068	13
Colorado		1	95	90	4	713	1	105	28		375	74	42	895	200	175	139	814	956	11	1
Connecticut	33	50	101	25	2	124	1	54	38		958	79	150	1,318	336	2,699	1,403	2,299	7,845	2	
Delaware			1			10			1		78		2	30	7	92	138	64	487		
District of Columbia	18	2	1	12	70	29	3	5	17	1	199	1	101	205	64	316	142	111	684	33	2
Florida	1,171	6	13	3		1	3,084	1	12		203	5	14	36	394	31	17	22	484	5	
Georgia	2						10		4		53	3	8	72	162	221	22	25	29		
Hawaii				1	106				5		81	1	2	39	1		2		1	9,051	98
Idaho		2	2	2	2	1		1	15		95	30	9	142	32	1	14	35	53	28	
Illinois	8	100	3,720	2,152	12	5,835	11	1,188	1,840	4	2,153	323	433	8,872	2,817	7,913	2,285	4,293	9,809	42	
Indiana	1	1	35	749		429	13	17	293		278	17	140	683	198	391	151	303	400	3	
Indian Territory			24			6			1		15		13	9	3	10	1	157	61		
Iowa	1	2	243	9		102		1	394		369	7	27	1,024	84	304	160	117	137	2	
Kansas			128	4		298			50		225		204	993	61	47	43	245	93	3	
Kentucky	3	1	2	2		2	1		6		92		10	213	15	227	55	14	34		
Louisiana	18	3	6		5	74	93	11	52	1	119	20	284	118	56	142	23	103	1,615	1	1
Maine	9	30		12		3	1	5	1		342	173	18	31	138	208	263	99	476	2	
Maryland	19	8	384	95	18	281	7	1	16	1	287	2	61	1,431	96	3,173	215	132	1,022		
Massachusetts	407	523	61	109	90	39	6	3	436	6	5,129	2,219	615	1,285	3,879	9,052	7,530	2,714	15,375	39	3
Michigan	5	35	217	307		1,226	1	24	1,902		1,660	3,837	92	2,238	150	1,051	259	1,699	2,077	7	
Minnesota		1	288	149	5	1,488		95	217	2	549	2,359	50	1,299	77	989	150	420	779	6	
Mississippi	1			3	4	33	23	16	14		24	9	7	23	17	25	1	399	438	1	
Missouri		32	375	801	10	1,857	7	216	175		319	6	104	2,838	2,326	1,941	439	946	1,861	13	
Montana			11	51	5	239		43	11		310	187	36	153	4	28	293	176	63	14	
Nebraska	1		629	16		60		1	69		112	4	15	1,488	83	234	98	44	264	1	
Nevada			1	8		32		13			28	2	60	39	1	7	19	337	44		
New Hampshire	1	22	2	8	1	1			1		217	128	17	45	1,274	154	246	54	125		
New Jersey	106	100	211	86	3	377	12	195	825	27	2,144	221	281	5,538	326	5,132	2,473	1,683	14,516	28	1
New Mexico			4	30		99		1	11		34	8	12	18	1	1	5	100	15	10	
New York	1,645	668	1,997	1,445	62	3,380	2,119	1,256	1,633	67	14,562	1,862	4,715	22,937	6,150	95,261	15,355	12,984	117,119	342	2
North Carolina	1						6				58	1	4	20	16	40	11	31	10	1	

TABLE VII.—IMMIGRANT ALIENS ADMITTED INTO THE UNITED STATES DURING THE FISCAL YEAR ENDED JUNE 30, 1906, SHOWING DESTINATIONS BY RACES OR PEOPLES—Continued.

State.	African (black).	Armenian.	Bohemian and Moravian (Czech).	Bulgarian, Servian, and Montenegrin.	Chinese.	Croatian and Slovenian.	Cuban.	Dalmatian, Bosnian, and Herzegovinian.	Dutch and Flemish.	East Indian.	English.	Finnish.	French.	German.	Greek.	Hebrew.	Irish.	Italian (north).	Italian (south).	Japanese.	Korean.
North Dakota			91			9		1	74		200	61	10	2,516	18	112	53	1	14	2	
Ohio	1	7	1,420	1,671	2	4,098	3	129	106	51	1,366	459	189	7,181	316	3,441	820	616	6,102	10	
Oklahoma			65	3		1			3		27		2	163	1	6	3				
Oregon			6	5	38	99		13	45	24	117	183	24	442	111	203	87	129	129	398	
Pennsylvania	83	75	1,062	2,789	8	19,341	34	336	214	3	5,777	343	765	13,289	1,520	16,685	5,649	7,010	47,395	11	
Philippine Islands											2			1							
Porto Rico	107						62		22	2	19		98	34	1	5		40	81	1	
Rhode Island	71	174	11	18	5	7		4	85		1,439	46	278	162	173	716	885	187	3,120	1	
South Carolina	1						3		52		7	15	3	28	17	27	5	6	17		
South Dakota			46	20		22		60	94		103	75	4	1,064	4	11	17	40	1		
Tennessee	1		3		1	183	8	4	2		70		5	82	51	274	9	165	36	3	
Texas	1		1,082	173	1	468	10	13	58		319	26	102	880	43	228	74	221	229	438	3
Utah				1	3	223		2	95		507	118	32	279	353	4	59	341	205	2	
Vermont	1			6		6			11		151	68	21	43	16	106	72	241	266		
Virginia	9	5	26	48	3	136	8	2	7		179	13	11	102	149	262	52	84	195	1	
Washington	4	2	22	51	102	400		124	144	57	624	383	120	838	80	144	209	602	716	1,619	3
West Virginia			54	225		711	2	113	15		172	18	26	239	219	60	33	337	2,904		
Wisconsin		2	447	111	8	1,228	2	42	487		335	326	41	3,765	664	1,102	89	424	764	1	
Wyoming	1		12	15		88		16			205	143	29	42	20		32	167	57	3	
Grand total	3,786	1,895	12,958	11,548	1,485	44,272	5,591	4,568	9,735	271	45,079	14,136	10,379	86,813	23,127	153,748	40,959	46,286	240,528	14,243	127

TABLE VII.—IMMIGRANT ALIENS ADMITTED INTO THE UNITED STATES DURING THE FISCAL YEAR ENDED JUNE 30, 1906, SHOWING DESTINATIONS BY RACES OR PEOPLES—Continued.

State.	Lithuanian.	Magyar.	Mexican.	Pacific Islander.	Polish.	Portuguese.	Roumanian.	Russian.	Ruthenian (Russniak).	Scandinavian (Norwegians, Danes, and Swedes).	Scotch.	Slovak.	Spanish.	Spanish-American.	Syrian.	Turkish.	Welsh.	West Indian (other than Cuban).	Other peoples.	Grand total.
Alabama		8	10		7					144	60	30	33	8	26	1	13	45		1,471
Alaska										20	11									139
Arizona	1	5			2					53	20	3	119		13		2			1,086
Arkansas	4				8			3		15	1	7		4	7					411
California	48	41	11	5	42	1,018	11	563	21	1,571	568	30	341	171	41	13	54	9	32	20,649
Colorado	3	33			94	2	1	11	1	486	164	92	8		24		47		6	5,691
Connecticut	910	1,738			4,303	62	70	171	426	1,257	345	918	3	1	109	30	22	10	50	27,942
Delaware	10	23			565		1	4	68	12	7	11					1			1,612
District of Columbia	3	14	1		7	2		27		32	72	4	19	39	11	3	3	5	1	2,259
Florida	3	1	12					4		40	25	1	1,088	10	36	4	1	151		6,878
Georgia	1	1			3	1		2		12	21	1	7	3	39	4	6	1		713
Hawaii	3					5		1		2	45						1			9,445
Idaho		4			2	5				226	16	4	100				4		22	847
Illinois	2,653	2,227			14,445	5	411	330	407	7,587	888	3,273	20	2	107	219	85		70	86,539
Indiana	100	896			777		1,326	1	28	154	143	343	2	11	222	181	31	2	41	8,360
Indian Territory	16	8			10				5	1	12	5	3		2		4			366
Iowa	19	37			62	1	3	7	6	2,023	99	17	1		47	1	44			5,350
Kansas	8	4			97		1	4	4	287	61	33	23		37	1	9	1		2,964
Kentucky		9			12		4	9	1	1	7	5	5		19	2	2		1	754
Louisiana	1		12		3	3	2	6		197	21	17	80	48	71	1		2		3,209
Maine	121	10			153	7	3	7		221	153	40	6	2	51	24	12	1	77	2,699
Maryland	285	162			1,257		93	356	104	119	136	181	5	4	15	4	12	10	1	9,993
Massachusetts	2,050	75	3		7,788	6,042	36	339	353	3,723	1,998	202	75	13	941	330	71	76	228	73,863
Michigan	177	1,033			4,191	1	129	16	53	1,883	403	401	4		136	24	21		12	25,271
Minnesota	18	55			624		14	29	55	8,377	155	191	3	1	62	14	38	2	7	18,568
Mississippi					1			2	1	48	8	5	11		53	6				1,173
Missouri	78	535	1		759	1	391	25	131	226	158	493	75	4	185	150	15	5	52	17,550
Montana		1			23		8		2	509	176	47	2		5		33			2,430
Nebraska	15	21			165		7	7	1	1,139	37	12		1	45		20			4,589
Nevada						30				30	8	1	123	1			2		38	824
New Hampshire	123	5			506	18	4	30	44	158	65	5			87	36	1	9	24	3,411
New Jersey	771	6,632			8,468	3	264	143	1,692	1,483	1,000	3,397	15	16	105	12	63	49	17	58,415
New Mexico	2	3			6		1	1		23	24	3	10		4		1			427
New York	2,250	9,905	84	7	20,602	433	715	2,015	3,626	11,724	5,531	5,338	2,181	966	1,584	480	600	876	230	374,708
North Carolina										7	14				37		2		4	263
North Dakota	3	19			124		49	125	61	2,836	103	10			21	1	4	1	5	6,524

TABLE VII.—IMMIGRANT ALIENS ADMITTED INTO THE UNITED STATES DURING THE FISCAL YEAR ENDED JUNE 30, 1906, SHOWING DESTINATIONS BY RACES OR PEOPLES—Continued.

State.	Lithuanian.	Magyar.	Mexican.	Pacific Islander.	Polish.	Portuguese.	Roumanian.	Russian.	Ruthenian (Russniak).	Scandinavian (Norwegians, Danes, and Swedes).	Scotch.	Slovak.	Spanish.	Spanish-American.	Syrian.	Turkish.	Welsh.	West Indian (other than Cuban).	Other peoples.	Grand total.
Ohio	279	6,130			3,390	26	4,454	40	552	473	466	3,035	8	9	269	120	128	1	29	47,397
Oklahoma	3				3		1			18	9	3	2	4	7					324
Oregon	2	18			10	9		2	5	543	83	31	4		18	2	5		1	2,786
Pennsylvania	3,771	13,222			22,561	13	2,919	1,197	8,243	1,833	1,953	18,591	38	44	804	271	707	69	56	198,681
Philippine Islands											4		4							11
Porto Rico			3		1	2		1		7	13	1	599	199	55	2		122	6	1,483
Rhode Island	64	6			771	1,020		19	84	387	293	17	3		101	28	28	10	2	10,215
South Carolina	1				1			4		5	32				11					235
South Dakota	3	6			10			11	2	1,204	11	2	1		24	1	16			2,852
Tennessee	1	5			7		2			7	86	18			9		6	1	1	1,040
Texas	1	64	4		604	2	3	106	124	224	61	30	144	12	174	3	5	13	2	5,945
Utah		1		1	1		2			431	58	9	6		7		10		1	2,751
Vermont	43	103			536	7	20	12	51	118	289	99	69		13		68			2,436
Virginia	5	188			35	6	15	28	6	51	84	45	26	2	45	8	6	2	1	1,845
Washington	21	24			204	3	36	86	4	2,468	256	28	22	9	15	11	47		4	9,482
West Virginia	128	607			629	2	420	39	74	20	40	439	35		109	23	47		1	7,741
Wisconsin	259	376			1,915		7	31	20	3,600	85	739	9	1	21	7	52	1	5	16,966
Wyoming		6			51		2		2	126	85	14				16	18	2		1,152
Grand total	14,257	44,261	141	13	95,835	8,729	11,425	5,814	16,257	58,141	16,463	38,221	5,332	1,585	5,824	2,033	2,367	1,476	1,027	1,100,735

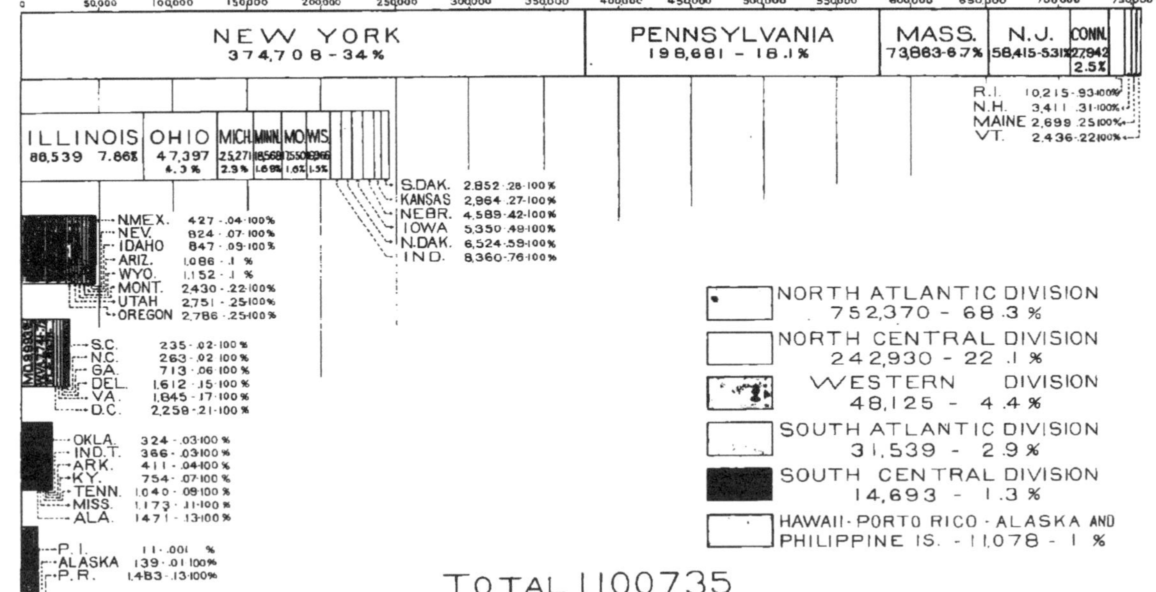

CHART 3. For further information see page 27
Bureau of Immigration and Naturalization
PROPORTION OF IMMIGRATION AND NUMBER OF IMMIGRANTS
GOING TO EACH STATE DURING THE FISCAL YEAR ENDED JUNE 30, 1906.
0
50,000
100,000
150,000
200,000
250,000
300,000
350,000
400,000
450,000
500,000
550,000
600,000
650,000
700,000
750,000
NEW YORK
374,708 - 34%
PENNSYLVANIA
198,681 - 18.1%
MASS.
73,863-6.7%
N.J.
58,415-5.31%
CONN.
27,942
2.5%
R.I. 10,215 .93 100%
N.H. 3,411 .31 100%
MAINE 2,699 .25 100%
VT. 2,436 .22 100%
ILLINOIS
86,539 7.86%
OHIO
47,397
4.3%
MICH.
25,271
2.3%
MINN.
18,568
1.69%
MO.
17,550
1.6%
WIS.
16,966
1.5%
S.DAK. 2,852 .28 100%
KANSAS 2,964 .27 100%
NEBR. 4,589 .42 100%
IOWA 5,350 .49 100%
N.DAK. 6,524 .59 100%
IND. 8,360 .76 100%
N.MEX. 427 .04 100%
NEV. 824 .07 100%
IDAHO 847 .09 100%
ARIZ. 1,086 .1 %
WYO. 1,152 .1 %
MONT. 2,430 .22 100%
UTAH 2,751 .25 100%
OREGON 2,786 .25 100%
S.C. 235 .02 100%
N.C. 263 .02 100%
GA. 713 .06 100%
DEL. 1,612 .15 100%
VA. 1,845 .17 100%
D.C. 2,258 .21 100%
OKLA. 324 .03 100%
IND.T. 366 .03 100%
ARK. 411 .04 100%
KY. 754 .07 100%
TENN. 1,040 .09 100%
MISS. 1,173 .11 100%
ALA. 1471 .13 100%
P.I. 11 .001 %
ALASKA 139 .01 100%
P.R. 1,483 .13 100%
NORTH ATLANTIC DIVISION
752,370 - 68.3%
NORTH CENTRAL DIVISION
242,930 - 22.1%
WESTERN DIVISION
48,125 - 4.4%
SOUTH ATLANTIC DIVISION
31,539 - 2.9%
SOUTH CENTRAL DIVISION
14,693 - 1.3%
HAWAII - PORTO RICO - ALASKA AND
PHILIPPINE IS. - 11,078 - 1%
TOTAL 1,100,735

CHART 4. FOR FURTHER INFORMATION SEE PAGE 27 BUREAU OF IMMIGRATION AND NATURALIZATION

PER CENT OF IMMIGRATION FOR LAST 8 YEARS, TO EACH STATE AND TERRITORY, BY RACE

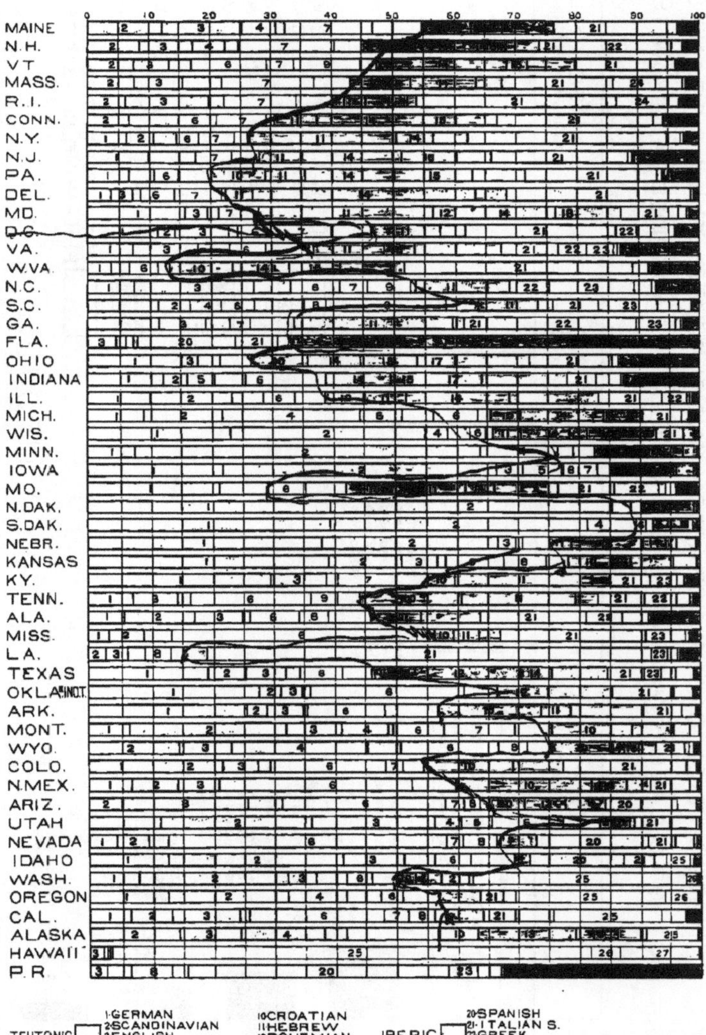

TEUTONIC: 1 GERMAN, 2 SCANDINAVIAN, 3 ENGLISH, 4 FINNISH, 5 DUTCH

KELTIC: 6 ITALIAN N., 7 IRISH, 8 FRENCH, 9 SCOTCH

SLAVIC: 10 CROATIAN, 11 HEBREW, 12 BOHEMIAN, 13 BULGARIAN, 14 POLISH, 15 SLOVAK, 16 DALMATIAN, 17 ROUMANIAN, 18 LITHUANIAN, 19 RUSSIAN

IBERIC: 20 SPANISH, 21 ITALIAN S., 22 GREEK, 23 SYRIAN, 24 PORTUGUESE

MONGOLIAN: 25 JAPANESE, 26 CHINESE, 27 KOREAN

ALL OTHERS: 28 AFRICAN, 29 CUBAN, 30 MAGYAR, 31 WEST INDIAN

Chart 3 (heretofore arranged differently and numbered 4) is designed to show graphically the proportion of immigration to the different States and sections of the country during the fiscal year 1906. The enormous proportion going to New York, Pennsylvania, and the North Atlantic section shows prominently.

The North Atlantic and North Central States together received 90 per cent of the entire immigration, the North Atlantic States getting 68 per cent and the North Central States 22 per cent. The entire South received but 4 per cent of the total immigration, 3 per cent going to the South Atlantic States and 1 per cent to the South Central States. The Western States received but 4 per cent. These proportions were the same during the fiscal year 1905. (See also Chart 4.)

Chart 4 shows the character of the immigration to each State with regard to race during the past eight years.

Grand division of race is shown by the color of the bars. The subdivision of race is indicated by the figures on the bars.

In view of the fact that the States having small immigration have as much color as those having heavy immigration, the total amount of color on the chart representing each grand division of race should not be taken as an index of the proportion of aliens of that race for the whole country.

TABLE VIII.—IMMIGRANT ALIENS ADMITTED INTO THE UNITED STATES DURING THE FISCAL YEAR ENDED JUNE 30, 1906, SHOWING OCCUPATIONS BY RACES OR PEOPLES.

Occupation.	African (black).	Armenian.	Bohemian and Moravian (Czech).	Bulgarian, Servian, and Montenegrin.	Chinese.	Croatian and Slovenian.	Cuban.	Dalmatian, Bosnian, and Herzegovinian.	Dutch and Flemish.	East Indian.	English.	Finnish.	French.	German.	Greek.	Hebrew.	Irish.	Italian (north).	Italian (south).	Japanese.	Korean.
PROFESSIONAL OCCUPATIONS.																					
Actors	2	7	1	......	......	4	55	......	11	......	483	1	58	142	1	23	34	57	34	27	....
Architects	1	2	1	......	......	1	......	......	13	......	124	......	30	102	1	25	12	7	9	4	....
Clergy	14	7	8	5	......	4	4	1	44	4	196	8	91	146	9	52	155	36	77	26	1
Editors	......	2	2	......	......	......	6	......	6	1	73	4	12	23	3	10	15	5	9	13	....
Electricians	2	2	4	1	......	1	4	......	11	......	136	1	16	86	......	71	31	18	33	1	....
Engineers (professional)	6	4	11	1	......	2	15	1	74	3	688	9	221	445	5	45	57	47	26	18	....
Lawyers	2	......	3	......	......	1	81	......	11	2	116	......	16	34	8	3	11	12	28	2	....
Literary and scientific persons	1	2	5	2	......	5	13	......	12	2	153	3	23	143	2	48	11	7	15	4	....
Musicians	5	......	44	1	......	4	7	......	50	......	128	......	109	256	26	227	54	108	334	......	....
Officials (government)	4	1	......	......	78	2	20	......	9	......	135	......	30	84	2	1	14	12	12	44	2
Physicians	5	1	3	......	1	2	56	......	8	3	135	6	28	129	11	40	20	18	73	16	....
Sculptors and artists	......	1	9	......	......	1	11	......	32	1	169	......	127	227	7	43	6	131	68	15	....
Teachers	32	16	8	4	8	1	18	1	20	3	293	8	329	369	13	333	134	45	56	53	2
Other professional	15	2	3	1	......	......	3	2	5	3	221	4	39	166	10	173	51	20	26	33	....
Total	89	47	102	15	87	28	293	5	306	22	3,050	44	1,129	2,352	98	1,094	605	523	800	256	5
SKILLED OCCUPATIONS.																					
Bakers	13	16	169	17	2	40	12	4	139	......	160	12	80	978	114	1,102	75	225	777	9	....
Barbers and hairdressers	8	23	34	14	1	13	22	2	15	......	63	1	32	503	64	594	21	104	2,563	13	....
Blacksmiths	28	31	204	28	......	104	......	10	57	......	233	21	43	763	64	840	187	169	1,177	3	....
Bookbinders	1	2	14	......	......	3	1	......	5	......	25	1	3	50	......	587	7	5	11	1	....
Brewers	......	......	35	......	......	2	......	......	8	......	23	......	1	244	......	37	6	5	......	......	....
Butchers	3	10	293	12	......	33	2	4	79	......	234	2	44	1,017	39	1,237	67	72	320	......	....
Cabinetmakers	1	2	9	7	......	10	......	......	7	......	65	......	8	102	3	677	20	11	47	1	....
Carpenters and joiners	121	40	430	24	......	147	20	11	275	......	1,444	120	83	1,666	146	4,785	479	501	2,746	39	....
Clerks and accountants	99	13	159	21	6	32	159	13	112	......	1,760	30	268	1,730	317	2,288	1,238	197	333	65	....
Dressmakers	56	6	60	4	1	15	1	4	22	......	311	6	214	310	2	2,271	494	187	1,019	......	....
Engineers (locomotive, marine, and stationary)	9	5	16	1	1	9	9	7	29	1	461	12	61	223	47	77	135	45	61	5	....

Engravers	1	1							2		22		6	25	1	48	6	9	5	1	
Furriers and fur workers			5	13		4		1			30		9	39	21	530	3		2		
Gardeners	1	1	24	36	1	11			112		256	2	40	248	20	38	84	47	211	10	
Hat and cap makers	1		5			7	4		1		26		7	39	2	718	3	19	41	1	
Iron and steel workers	2	38	67	1		11	3		17		473	22	22	251	8	75	151	42	72	1	
Jewelers	1	6	3	1		1	2		14		44	2	20	42	1	181	3	11	27		
Locksmiths		3	233	14		44			4		9	3	18	877	2	1,314		41	5		
Machinists	1	5	28	3		21	6	1	25		394	18	58	281	17	193	113	58	110	5	
Mariners	247	5	10	4		256	8	191	93	2	455	267	71	412	622	75	123	185	1,735	36	
Masons	30	16	229	23		163	1	30	82		1,318	16	26	775	58	431	298	1,694	4,449		
Mechanics (not specified)	19	3	10	1		8	37		16		213	4	84	213	8	121	39	63	283	1	
Metal workers (other than iron, steel, and tin)	2	9	8	1	1	1	3		13		135	5	16	95	7	403	11	15	114	1	
Millers	1		59	6		15			17		21		10	259	4	138	11	25	219		
Milliners	14		1			2			1		48		30	42	4	488	56	12	23		
Miners	2	1	259	50		248		20	59		2,012	106	299	613	16	45	342	1,812	655	11	
Painters and glaziers	9	9	50	3		10	12	1	88	1	339	15	43	398	21	2,297	65	74	300	7	2
Photographers	2	2	2	1			4		7	1	30	1	4	44		219	3	2	35	13	
Plasterers	2		1				3		9		381	1	4	18		17	105	19	27		
Plumbers	2	1	2				1	1	6		281	1	1	10		77	63	3	5		
Printers	14	1	12	4		5	7	1	19		144	4	17	151	13	393	39	17	77	5	
Saddlers and harness makers	13	1	41	3		7	2		3		47	1	7	130	1	256	27	3	35		
Seamstresses	241	9	72	2		13			22		53	18	31	252	10	3,574	177	85	1,355	1	
Shipwrights	3					1			2		89		3	2		1	12	1			
Shoemakers	57	126	261	40		102		6	41		160	26	29	736	119	2,353	78	410	6,089	9	
Stokers	5		4	1		4		4	4		49	3	1	44	22	2	33	11	46		
Stonecutters	2	3	35			12		3	7		204	10	15	117	6	21	64	312	515	4	
Tailors	61	84	365	40	5	94	10	19	46	1	175	79	41	940	144	18,418	113	321	3,998	22	
Tanners and curriers		4	13	6		10		1	7		27	7	6	95	15	254	10	11	29		
Textile workers (not specified)		3	1			2			3	6	340	3	13	88	3	113	97	14	38		
Tinners	1	2	31	3		6	1		4		30	3	8	203	4	832	3	4	102		
Tobacco workers	233	1	8		1		1,254		128		24		1	43	26	560	3	5	9		
Upholsterers		1	1	2					5		39		11	60	2	228	7	4	13		
Watch and clock makers	2	8	8	1					3		26	5	32	76	5	720	4	11	56	6	
Weavers and spinners	1	31	61	1		5			104		953	6	188	469	5	507	244	198	206	19	
Wheelwrights	12		49	9		14			6		31		1	163	1	51	3	3	6		
Woodworkers (not specified)	3	2	44	1		7	1		8		50	4	7	131	5	213	17	6	81	9	
Other skilled	8	11	60	9		10	5	2	31		771	20	118	413	32	742	201	102	364	31	
Total	1,332	535	3,485	407	19	1,502	1,590	336	1,757	12	14,478	857	2,134	16,380	2,021	51,141	5,340	7,170	30,391	329	2
MISCELLANEOUS OCCUPATIONS.																					
Agents	3	3	3		3	2	7	1	28		368	2	46	65	7	82	50	15	12	1	
Bankers							8		16		202		26	52	2	10	7	4	17	7	
Draymen, hackmen, and teamsters	1		18	1		4	8		10		112	2	30	69	4	44	59	84	506	1	
Farm laborers	220	280	1,514	5,736	18	21,808	5	1,424	1,054	2	515	901	367	12,307	4,615	1,712	2,195	6,132	73,567	8,435	58

TABLE VIII.—IMMIGRANT ALIENS ADMITTED INTO THE UNITED STATES DURING THE FISCAL YEAR ENDED JUNE 30, 1906, SHOWING OCCUPATIONS BY RACES OR PEOPLES—Continued.

Occupation.	African (black).	Armenian.	Bohemian and Moravian (Czech).	Bulgarian, Servian, and Montenegrin.	Chinese.	Croatian and Slovenian.	Cuban.	Dalmatian, Bosnian, and Herzegovinian.	Dutch and Flemish.	East Indian.	English.	Finnish.	French.	German.	Greek.	Hebrew.	Irish.	Italian (north).	Italian (south).	Japanese.	Korean.
MISCELLANEOUS OCCUPATIONS—Continued.																					
Farmers	67	69	218	792	3	906	9	198	510	19	608	78	330	1,890	772	168	1,002	1,502	914	522	....
Fishermen	1	....	....	....	1	2	3	17	3	....	6	6	3	6	27	10	12	7	214	6	....
Hotel keepers	1	....	2	2	2	1	1	....	5	1	63	....	25	79	22	29	43	23	21	47	....
Laborers	436	226	531	3,935	183	13,108	134	2,284	1,286	42	2,512	7,075	451	6,592	12,975	8,378	10,160	17,565	70,344	835	1
Manufacturers	....	....	3	....	....	1	5	....	15	....	300	2	71	107	9	47	44	21	28	21	....
Merchants and dealers	21	53	63	26	662	33	465	9	302	34	1,540	14	586	2,904	443	3,495	307	638	2,016	632	7
Servants	700	162	2,025	110	116	2,722	258	98	462	8	3,153	2,955	1,496	11,794	546	9,839	14,992	3,157	10,840	195	2
Other miscellaneous	50	15	21	1	167	8	56	1	95	82	1,342	23	129	497	74	556	571	139	435	510	5
Total	1,500	808	4,398	10,603	1,155	38,595	959	4,032	3,786	188	10,721	11,058	3,560	36,362	19,496	24,370	29,442	29,287	158,914	11,212	73
No occupation (including women and children)	865	505	4,973	523	224	4,147	2,749	195	3,886	49	16,830	2,177	3,556	31,719	1,512	77,143	5,572	9,306	50,423	2,446	47
Grand total	3,786	1,895	12,958	11,548	1,485	44,272	5,591	4,568	9,735	271	45,079	14,136	10,379	86,813	23,127	153,748	40,959	46,286	240,528	14,243	127

TABLE VIII.—IMMIGRANT ALIENS ADMITTED INTO THE UNITED STATES DURING THE FISCAL YEAR ENDED JUNE 30, 1906, SHOWING OCCUPATIONS BY RACES OR PEOPLES—Continued.

Occupation.	Lithuanian.	Magyar.	Mexican.	Pacific Islander.	Polish.	Portuguese.	Roumanian.	Russian.	Ruthenian (Russniak).	Scandinavian (Norwegians, Danes, and Swedes).	Scotch.	Slovak.	Spanish.	Spanish-American.	Syrian.	Turkish.	Welsh.	West Indian (other than Cuban).	Other peoples.	Grand total.
PROFESSIONAL OCCUPATIONS.																				
Actors		6	2	3	1		3	10		21	19	3	69	33		5	2			1,117
Architects	3	6			8	1	1	5		40	40		4	1		1	1	1		444
Clergy	5	16	1		27	5	2	7	6	48	47	7	37	9	18	13	22	4	4	1,166
Editors		4			2			2		14	9		2	4	2		2	1		226
Electricians		8	1		9	1		2	1	86	26	1	10	2			5	2	1	573
Engineers (professional)		26	2		22	6	4	20	1	292	222	4	15	16		1	9	6		2,324
Lawyers		4			3		1	1		10	19		20	26			1	7		422
Literary and scientific persons		14			5	2	1	7		29	27		3	7	3		5		1	555
Musicians	6	27	1		46	2	2	8	1	30	17	2	5	5			4	2		1,511
Officials (government)		20	1		1	4		26		32	19	1	18	35		2	1	12	2	624
Physicians		6	5		8	5	5	13	1	52	25		6	24	4	2	5	8	1	725
Sculptors and artists	1	22	2		17	2	4	24	2	27	24	3	36	7	1	4	4			1,028
Teachers	9	30			20		1	13	5	107	72	3	14	8	17	1	12	12	1	2,071
Other professional	1	9			22	1	1	8	1	56	65	1	4	10	2		8	13	1	980
Total	25	198	15	3	191	29	25	146	18	844	631	25	243	187	47	29	81	68	11	13,766
SKILLED OCCUPATIONS.																				
Bakers	12	68			196	3	15	9	3	263	135	24	52	1	7	14	10	2	2	4,760
Barbers and hairdressers	2	86			32	6	6	1		62	10	6	17	3	20	9	2	5	4	4,361
Blacksmiths	58	313			542	4	27	26	51	517	125	121	14	2	49	7	19	10	1	5,848
Bookbinders	1	11			9			1		32	8	2		1				2		783
Brewers	1	2			9					15	4	2	1			1	1			397
Butchers	3	181			246	1	6	4	10	140	68	44	4		3	4	6	3	3	4,194
Cabinetmakers	20	14			58	2		10	2	31	47	3			8				2	1,167
Carpenters and joiners	137	454	1		813	56	33	98	66	1,778	1,117	167	72	4	128	13	93	37	41	18,185
Clerks and accountants	15	143	3		149	32	11	31	6	876	576	29	303	54	59	21	78	114	5	11,345
Dressmakers	18	107			122	4	13	16	4	174	89	12	10		46		12	22	3	5,635
Engineers (locomotive, marine, and stationary)	12	27	1		31	15	3	6		376	212	6	200	9	1	1	23	6		2,143

TABLE VIII.—IMMIGRANT ALIENS ADMITTED INTO THE UNITED STATES DURING THE FISCAL YEAR ENDED JUNE 30, 1906, SHOWING OCCUPATIONS BY RACES OR PEOPLES—Continued.

Occupation.	Lithuanian.	Magyar.	Mexican.	Pacific Islander.	Polish.	Portuguese.	Roumanian.	Russian.	Ruthenian (Russniak).	Scandinavian (Norwegians, Danes, and Swedes).	Scotch.	Slovak.	Spanish.	Spanish-American.	Syrian.	Turkish.	Welsh.	West Indian (other than Cuban).	Other peoples.	Grand total.
SKILLED OCCUPATIONS—continued.																				
Engravers		2			4	1			1	7	9		1				1	2	1	156
Furriers and fur workers	1	16			15		7	2	4	11	2	9				5	2			731
Gardeners	7	37			67		2	1	2	125	120	13	3		3	3	11		1	1,537
Hat and cap makers	4	7			12	1	3	3	1	4	5	5	3						1	923
Iron and steel workers	41	45			115		1	2	4	164	257	39	32	2	6	1	15		1	1,981
Jewelers	1	4			3			2		13	3				6	1	1	1		394
Locksmiths	56	242			400	1	7	24	14	6		86	3				1			3,407
Machinists	13	51			40	1	6	7	2	292	184	7	10	3	2	1	8	1	2	1,967
Mariners	23	12	4	6	18	57	3	24		3,269	125	11	206	32	4	14	22	94	16	8,737
Masons	34	145			295	13	11	10	26	363	923	88	39		60	9	90	9	25	11,779
Mechanics (not specified)	6	23	2		28		1	8	3	111	55	4	36	2	3	2	3	5		1,415
Metal workers (other than iron, steel, and tin)	2	13			21			3	1	52	47	5	1	1	9		1	2	1	999
Millers	6	64			104	2	1	1	4	51	3	37	1	2			2		1	1,064
Milliners	2	3			5		4	4		8	16		1	1	1		2	3		771
Miners	300	49	1		389	6	16	6	6	193	620	93	52	3	3		429		1	8,717
Painters and glaziers	12	69			109	5	2	13	2	363	146	16	12		5	3	14	7	9	4,531
Photographers	2	5			4	1	1	4		44	6	2		2	2	1	1	1		446
Plasterers	1									3	531		3				36	2		1,163
Plumbers		1			3					14	188		2				7	4		673
Printers	2	26			18	1		11	4	57	54	6	6		3		2	7	1	1,121
Saddlers and harness makers	3	24			63	1	3	2	1	41	9	10	2				2	7		745
Seamstresses	9	44	1		203	21	4	2	1	354	12	20	2	4	42	1	5	56	3	6,699
Shipwrights						1				22	14	1	1				2			155
Shoemakers	57	373	1		645	12	26	25	73	243	32	283	10	17	141	9	4	16	13	12,622
Stokers	8	4			13	4	2	3	2	80	31	3	331		1	1	5	1	7	729
Stonecutters	1	7			21	5				148	447	4	68		19	2	57		3	2,112
Tailors	156	308			671	5	25	103	74	300	73	143	20	11	63	23	5	14	12	26,982
Tanners and curriers	3	22			23		5	1	4	25	13	46		3	4	2	2		1	649
Textile workers (not specified)					22		1	1	1	19	107	3	1		10					889

Tinners	7	44			68		3	4	2	45	20	26	3	1	1		15			1,476
Tobacco workers		7	2		4	1		2		27		3	316	1	5	4		2		2,670
Upholsterers		4			14					17	11	1		1		1		1	2	425
Watch and clock makers	3	9			12	2	1	5		38	7	3			2	1	1	1		1,048
Weavers and spinners	8	13			105	9		7	6	35	204	5	1	4	75	2	7		2	3,481
Wheelwrights	3	55			85		6	2	9	24	5	18					3			559
Woodworkers (not specified)	4	27			46		2	2	1	38	30	17	6			1	2			765
Other skilled	14	46			88	4	7	12	5	241	342	29	23	3	9	1	20	8	4	3,786
Total	1,068	3,207	16	6	5,940	277	264	498	395	11,111	7,042	1,452	1,868	167	800	158	1,022	445	168	177,122
MISCELLANEOUS OCCUPATIONS.																				
Agents		7	2		4	3	1	1		41	61		22	9	6	3	14	9		881
Bankers		2						1		2	41	1	9	7	1	1	1	1		418
Draymen, hackmen, and teamsters		15			10	2	1	1	2	39	55	1	6		3		2			1,090
Farm laborers	3,944	19,327			32,248	321	8,504	1,629	6,450	3,754	266	17,648	221	2	953	672	50	7	264	239,125
Farmers	78	269	2		760	86	86	86	120	1,412	191	541	153	36	579	156	68	38	50	15,288
Fishermen		3			7	174				362	7	1	18		1			1	1	899
Hotel keepers		2			4	2	2	1		14	11	2	10	2	3	1	1			422
Laborers	3,717	6,322	4		22,382	3,109	1,560	1,927	5,171	15,013	675	4,707	587	31	738	772	138	53	386	226,345
Manufacturers	2	10			9			1		25	58	4	9	2	3		4	1	1	803
Merchants and dealers	7	136	21		87	55	20	90	9	304	382	19	719	270	422	76	46	104	37	17,054
Servants	2,718	5,034	5		15,725	1,744	289	195	2,733	14,049	1,171	5,507	297	63	453	42	164	152	13	115,984
Other miscellaneous	9	27			70	13	7	15	1	382	616	10	49	14	14	4	48	21	1	6,078
Total	10,475	31,154	34		71,306	5,509	10,470	3,947	14,486	35,397	3,534	28,441	2,100	436	3,176	1,727	536	387	753	624,387
No occupation (including women and children)	2,689	9,702	76	4	18,398	2,914	666	1,223	1,358	10,789	5,256	8,303	1,121	795	1,801	119	728	576	95	285,460
Grand total	14,257	44,261	141	13	95,835	8,729	11,425	5,814	16,257	58,141	16,463	38,221	5,332	1,585	5,824	2,033	2,367	1,476	1,027	1,100,735

TABLE IX.—IMMIGRANT ALIENS ADMITTED INTO THE UNITED STATES DURING THE FISCAL YEAR ENDED JUNE 30, 1906, SHOWING DESTINATIONS AND OCCUPATIONS.

Occupation.	Alabama.	Alaska.	Arizona.	Arkansas.	California.	Colorado.	Connecticut.	Delaware.	District of Columbia.	Florida.	Georgia.	Hawaii.	Idaho.	Illinois.	Indiana.	Indian Territory.	Iowa.	Kansas.	Kentucky.
PROFESSIONAL OCCUPATIONS.																			
Actors					55	1	2			72				29	7				1
Architects	2				40	1	3	1				1		17	2		2		
Clergy	3		4	1	30	5	10	3	14	5	3	13		83	6	2	14	7	5
Editors		2			12	1			9	3		1		12	1				1
Electricians	1				20	4	11		1	5		1	2	50			1	2	
Engineers (professional)	2	4	13	2	108	15	25	4	19	9	1	4	2	91	6	3	4	2	1
Lawyers					18	3			8	5	1	1	1	11	1		1		
Literary and scientific persons		1	2	1	30	6	6	1	3	3	1	4		17	2		1	2	
Musicians	2		1		27	5	19	1	5	4	2	1	1	82	4		5	3	1
Officials (government)	2	1			43	3	3		144	10	2	4	1	16			1		
Physicians	1	2		1	22	1	3		5	6	3	3		35	3	1	1	3	2
Sculptors and artists	1				41	7	3		8	2				54	1			1	2
Teachers	4			2	55	9	40	1	17	7	5	16		143	7		18	6	1
Other professional	2				35	2	7	1	2	6	3	7	1	53	4	1	4	1	4
Total	20	10	20	7	536	63	132	12	235	137	21	56	8	693	44	7	52	27	18
SKILLED OCCUPATIONS.																			
Bakers	3		7	2	116	12	97	4	12	30	2	3	1	354	22	1	32	6	5
Barbers and hairdressers	3		1		33	4	119	1	10	38	2	4		203	5		3	3	1
Blacksmiths	2		16		45	19	147	8	7	7	2	3	4	557	37	2	35	22	7
Bookbinders					8		15		1	2	3			48			2	1	1
Brewers					6	2	4	2	2	1			1	46	2				1
Butchers	1		1	1	54	8	71	2	5	10			1	491	24	1	29	9	8
Cabinetmakers	4		2		16	2	20	5	4	2		1		115	5				1
Carpenters and joiners	21	3	25	11	335	39	417	17	38	81	11	8	13	1,323	66	6	92	21	15
Clerks and accountants	30	5	16	7	345	46	159	10	43	239	25	23	15	804	47	1	58	29	9
Dressmakers	5		3	3	67	14	130	3	15	7	2	1	6	287	14		22	6	6
Engineers (locomotive, marine, and stationary)	23	1	8	1	93	9	30	3	5	15	3	8	2	99	5	2	9	10	2
Engravers					3	1	2			2				7	1		1		
Furriers and fur workers				1	1		4		1					23	1				
Gardeners	3	1	2	1	60	10	40	3	4	5				109	11		10	7	4
Hat and cap makers			1		6	1	20			7				45	1	1	1		1
Iron and steel workers	5		8	3	29	9	66	3	2	7	4			169	8		11	5	2
Jewelers	3				10		4		2	2				17	2		1		
Locksmiths	2		1	1	19	8	61	9	2		1	1		334	16	1	3	6	10
Machinists	1			1	41	4	52	1	3	7		2	1	151	6	1	8	5	3
Mariners	111		12		854	17	96	3	6	423	20	3	8	298	5	1	15	6	
Masons	10		14	3	197	66	287	5	22	13	4		8	719	40	4	49	13	5

Mechanics (not specified)	3	1	1	1	18	7	53	1	1				2	65	8	1	3	4	
Metal workers (other than iron, steel, and tin)	1		2		14		37	1	3	3		1	2	46	5		2		
Millers	3	1	3		6	5	35	1		3			3	112	4		9	3	
Milliners	1				8		17	1	1		1			46					
Miners	39	22	316	24	236	299	83	16	13	3	2	1	22	869	177	36	101	173	19
Painters and glaziers	3				61	10	77	2	4	17	1	1		244	18	1	21	2	6
Photographers	1				11	2	6		2	2			1	29	1			3	
Plasterers					17	1	11		6	4				32	1		2		1
Plumbers					11	2	17		2	2	1			33	3				2
Printers	1				24	3	17		1	14	1	2		71	6		5	1	
Saddlers and harnessmakers			1	2	7		12		1	3			2	60	6		6	1	2
Seamstresses	3		2	1	33	7	151	2	5	56	7		2	423	18		25	5	3
Shipwrights					2		2	2						4	1			1	
Shoemakers	15		1	2	87	24	405	27	33	15	11			830	43	2	35	14	8
Stokers	12		1		5	1	9			1	2		2	19	5		2	1	
Stonecutters	1		14		39	8	47	1	1	3	14		3	84	6	1	7	2	
Tailors	5			1	111	29	431	19	44	39	13	6	3	1,444	54	1	48	12	19
Tanners and curriers	1				6	2	9	5			1			81	4		3	1	3
Textile workers (not specified)	7				6	3	20		1		1		2	29	1			2	1
Tinners	1				7	3	17	1	3	2			1	107	8		6	1	1
Tobacco workers	4				1	1	15			1,769	1		1	36	2		4		1
Upholsterers	1				9		7							26				1	
Watch and clock makers	1				12	4	28		2	2	2	1		55	4		7	3	1
Weavers and spinners	1		1		28	4	136	2	3			1	2	92	12	1	10	5	4
Wheelwrights					4		8		1	1				81	5		6	3	
Wood workers (not specified)	2				16	1	14			6			1	67	1	1	5	1	1
Other skilled	6		4		104	7	79	2	7	11	6	4	3	230	31		10	5	3
Total	339	34	463	66	3,221	694	3,584	162	318	2,854	143	74	112	11,414	742	65	698	393	156
MISCELLANEOUS OCCUPATIONS.																			
Agents	4				30	3	11		3	3	6	3		40	1	1	4	3	
Bankers	1		2		23	3	2		2	5		1	1	9					
Draymen, hackmen, and teamsters					17	10	19	2	4	8			2	68	3		6	3	2
Farm laborers	289	13	106	41	2,274	1,139	6,276	505	256	272	50	8,211	96	21,735	3,129	57	746	432	60
Farmers	12	4	57	14	1,045	180	262	5	21	74	13	18	52	1,426	314	18	344	141	21
Fishermen	3	2			28	2	8			21		4	6	35			9	1	
Hotel keepers		3	1		35	2	6	1	1	9	1	4	1	26	2		1	2	
Laborers	175	40	240	66	4,180	1,343	5,959	388	406	463	111	23	160	17,824	1,579	68	940	394	72
Manufacturers	1		1		26	1	12	1	1	7	1			40	4		3		2
Merchants and dealers	44	2	26	13	1,166	44	167	8	52	196	37	88	8	752	70	5	50	11	30
Servants	53	10	30	34	1,658	512	3,873	196	267	490	42	49	91	10,344	497	15	756	285	71
Other miscellaneous	14	2	6	4	695	34	91	5	11	50	2	12	14	302	30	1	38	6	4
Total	596	76	469	172	11,177	3,273	16,686	1,111	1,024	1,598	263	8,413	431	52,601	5,629	165	2,897	1,278	262
No occupation (including women and children)	516	19	134	166	5,715	1,661	7,540	327	682	2,289	286	902	296	21,831	1,945	129	1,703	1,266	318
Grand total	1,471	139	1,086	411	20,649	5,691	27,942	1,612	2,259	6,878	713	9,445	847	86,539	8,360	366	5,350	2,964	754

TABLE IX.—IMMIGRANT ALIENS ADMITTED INTO THE UNITED STATES DURING THE FISCAL YEAR ENDED JUNE 30, 1906, SHOWING DESTINATIONS AND OCCUPATIONS—Continued.

Occupation.	Louisiana.	Maine.	Maryland.	Massachusetts.	Michigan.	Minnesota.	Mississippi.	Missouri.	Montana.	Nebraska.	Nevada.	New Hampshire.	New Jersey.	New Mexico.	New York.	North Carolina.	North Dakota.	Ohio.	Oklahoma.
PROFESSIONAL OCCUPATIONS.																			
Actors	3		2	13	21	3		3					13		684			15	
Architects	1	2	8	29	6	3		4		1		1	20	1	240			6	
Clergy	22	3	11	75	21	38	3	18	9	11		1	32	5	424	2	14	35	2
Editors			1	9	2	2						1	11		138		1	1	
Electricians	2	1	8	47	18	7	1	7	2			1	28		255		1	13	
Engineers (professional)	8	6	19	95	38	22	1	19	8	1	2	2	51	1	1,419	3	2	38	
Lawyers	6	1	1	25	2	2			1	2		2	8		288	1	1	2	
Literary and scientific persons	1	1	1	31	10	4	1	7		2		1	32		295	2	2	8	
Musicians	102	4	22	75	27	5	2	11	2	6			55		802		1	36	
Officials (government)	5	2	3	16	5	1		9	1	1			8		297	1		5	
Physicians	3	2	12	31	7	9		7	3	2		3	16	2	389	1		14	1
Sculptors and artists	9	1	4	34	10	4		6	1	3			32		698	1		14	1
Teachers	9	3	32	185	19	37	2	22	2	8		5	88		959		5	60	
Other professional	5	1	21	39	14	5		9	1	4		4	28		551	1	1	23	
Total	176	27	145	704	200	142	10	122	30	41	2	21	422	9	7,439	12	28	270	4
SKILLED OCCUPATIONS.																			
Bakers	7	9	59	312	108	57	1	81	6	21	3	9	251		2,255		9	141	1
Barbers and hairdressers	12	10	37	299	43	20	1	67	1	6	1	4	234	1	2,561		4	102	
Blacksmiths	9	13	66	359	141	123		83	9	44	1	11	310	3	2,091	1	32	279	1
Bookbinders	1		7	36	10	7		3		1			18		502			15	
Brewers	2	1	9	13	10	5		21	1	2			19		157			19	
Butchers	8	5	69	204	87	47	1	83	7	27	1	9	218		1,888	1	12	167	2
Cabinetmakers	4		31	89	36	19		17	1	4		4	40		517	1	3	49	
Carpenters and joiners	37	35	213	1,078	379	357	6	221	36	71	7	30	1,026	4	8,531	4	134	538	4
Clerks and accountants	52	22	95	683	150	163	8	157	27	60	8	23	453	6	5,566	5	55	254	6
Dressmakers	22	15	81	408	59	46	1	46	11	20	4	9	267		3,028	4	8	110	
Engineers (locomotive, marine, and stationary)	28	10	18	135	50	28	1	17	8	5	4	2	122	2	914		5	67	1
Engravers	1		1	8		3	1	1					10		88			3	
Furriers and fur workers		1	7	31	5	3		7		1			16		548		1	14	
Gardeners	21	2	18	94	41	22	3	40	1	12		7	63		603		9	69	
Hat and cap makers	1	1	12	52	6	8		11					50		554		1	20	
Iron and steel workers	4	5	14	214	74	39		30	4	4	1	3	116	1	536		8	104	
Jewelers	4		7	18	2			1				2	14		247			7	
Locksmiths	3	2	74	123	57	22	1	49		14		2	203	1	1,460		4	194	1
Machinists	8	7	18	196	59	56		17	4	6	1	7	107		698		7	68	2

Mariners	86	20	83	532	78	65	23	76	9	13	9	7	323	1	4,262	1	25	64	
Masons	24	33	92	555	231	129	4	209	35	29	7	18	613	6	5,710	4	32	377	
Mechanics (not specified)	9	5	7	101	14	15	1	8	1	3	1	3	83		694		5	35	
Metal workers (other than iron, steel, and tin)	5	3	7	66	16	5		5		2		2	59		550		3	14	
Millers	3	1	14	46	23	21		19		8		3	56		367		10	63	1
Milliners	3	1	6	58	3	8		3		1			25		472	1		8	
Miners	5	18	69	199	656	155	1	110	207	18	33	8	144	21	987	4	49	308	3
Painters and glaziers	8	10	56	276	67	73		35	1	17	2	7	205		2,644		21	106	
Photographers	2	2	6	27	4	7		7					19		246		3	10	
Plasterers	5	2	4	41	19	7		3	1		1	1	42		855	2		5	
Plumbers			3	77	21	7		3	3	4		4	41		269	1	4	26	
Printers	1	2	13	62	28	13		11	2	1		2	55		603		7	21	1
Saddlers and harnessmakers	3	2	12	42	14	11		10	2	6			31		355		5	36	
Seamstresses	8	5	97	398	39	56	3	48	4	17	2	8	293	1	4,003	1	12	161	2
Shipwrights			1	13	4	3		1					11		53		1	7	
Shoemakers	45	25	125	1,040	169	87	8	150	4	54	2	34	804	1	5,726	2	33	380	1
Stokers	7	2	3	25	7	5		3	1				31		509		2	7	
Stonecutters	3	44	18	360	29	45		19	3	3	1	16	67	3	686		3	51	2
Tailors	24	32	482	1,707	173	175	5	272	12	43	1	35	995	1	16,722	2	28	550	1
Tanners and curriers	1	2	9	55	9	2		5	1	2		1	32		291			24	2
Textile workers (not specified)	2	19	5	248		4		8	1			18	68		245	5	2	19	
Tinners	5	1	39	80	17	14		19	1	3		2	71		799		5	52	
Tobacco workers	3	2	6	150	8	5		3		3		2	22	1	510			12	
Upholsterers	4	1	7	25	7	6		6	1	1		1	16		243		1	9	
Watch and clock makers	1	1	31	67	3	9		16		2		1	40		614		2	17	
Weavers and spinners	1	48	13	774	39	21	1	30	3	11		43	456	1	854	1	6	53	
Wheelwrights			10	14	14	6		4		9			39		177		5	35	1
Woodworkers (not specified)	1		7	40	16	11		18	1	4		2	44		336		3	33	
Other skilled	10	41	43	422	79	76		45	9	8		14	203	2	1,527	1	12	154	1
Total	493	460	2,104	11,852	3,104	2,066	70	2,098	418	560	90	354	8,425	56	84,053	41	571	4,857	33
MISCELLANEOUS OCCUPATIONS.																			
Agents	12		2	40	10	9		12	3	1			25		505		1	13	
Bankers	9		2	15	1	1	1			1	1	1	2		305	1	1		
Draymen, hackmen, and teamsters	2	1	5	83	20	11		9	2	8	2	2	52	1	523		3	19	2
Farm laborers	756	382	2,044	10,217	4,770	2,679	211	4,485	280	663	199	603	13,657	59	54,043	10	982	16,452	46
Farmers	48	38	53	790	434	473	18	519	184	198	87	43	475	26	3,190		296	534	15
Fishermen	1		4	94	35	81	1	11	7	3		1	23		222		43	3	
Hotel keepers	1	1	3	21	6	6		4	1	1	1		18		176		1	7	1
Laborers	295	828	1,059	18,610	7,500	6,149	155	4,436	668	768	241	1,385	9,929	111	67,296	17	1,273	8,700	19
Manufacturers	3	1	5	49	7	4		13	1	1	1		40	1	444		1	10	
Merchants and dealers	133	31	153	782	156	101	18	188	28	30	7	21	558	9	9,550	6	19	291	4
Servants	126	300	902	11,957	2,391	2,652	89	1,223	255	543	41	414	7,794	30	39,400	15	929	4,355	34
Other miscellaneous	21	28	25	523	116	77	3	56	23	20	6	14	278	7	2,331	2	16	175	2
Total	1,407	1,610	4,257	43,181	15,446	12,243	496	10,956	1,452	2,237	586	2,484	32,851	244	177,985	51	3,565	30,557	123
No occupation (including women and children)	1,133	602	3,487	18,126	6,521	4,117	597	4,374	530	1,751	146	552	16,717	118	105,231	159	2,360	11,713	164
Grand total	3,209	2,699	9,993	73,863	25,271	18,568	1,173	17,550	2,430	4,589	824	3,411	58,415	427	374,708	263	6,524	47,397	324

TABLE IX.—IMMIGRANT ALIENS ADMITTED INTO THE UNITED STATES DURING THE FISCAL YEAR ENDED JUNE 30, 1906, SHOWING DESTINATIONS AND OCCUPATIONS—Continued.

Occupation.	Oregon.	Pennsylvania.	Philippine Islands.	Porto Rico.	Rhode Island.	South Carolina.	South Dakota.	Tennessee.	Texas.	Utah.	Vermont.	Virginia.	Washington.	West Virginia.	Wisconsin.	Wyoming.	Grand total.
PROFESSIONAL OCCUPATIONS.																	
Actors		27		138	1				3		1	1	20		2		1,117
Architects	2	35		1	3				3		2	1	2		4		444
Clergy	7	100		20	12	1	3	5	38	4	5	9	11		17		1,166
Editors		9		1						1			6	1			226
Electricians		44		3	10		2		3			5	12	1	3	1	573
Engineers (professional)	3	155		19	12		1	4	22	5	2	5	19	4	23		2,324
Lawyers	1	11		12					2	1				1	1	1	422
Literary and scientific persons	2	47		6	3				3		1		6	2	7		555
Musicians	4	135		7	5	1	1		8	1	1	2	11		14	8	1,511
Officials (government)	5	15		3	2		2					2	8	1	1	1	624
Physicians	6	81		11	4	1	1	1	9	2		2	6		7		725
Sculptors and artists	3	42		4	4				6	3	1	3	6		18		1,028
Teachers	8	175	2	5	16	1	4	2	11	11	2	2	25	2	35	3	2,071
Other professional	7	81		8	7		1	2	6	1	1	3	15		7	1	980
Total	48	957	2	238	79	4	15	14	114	29	16	35	147	12	139	15	13,766
SKILLED OCCUPATIONS.																	
Bakers	10	452		8	34		12	3	39	10	7	4	40	12	87	3	4,760
Barbers and hairdressers	3	412		9	38		1		6	4	3	3	15	12	21	1	4,361
Blacksmiths	13	977		4	57	1	21	3	33	17	16	10	48	31	119	2	5,848
Bookbinders	2	81			4				2	1	2	2	1		7		783
Brewers	1	42			1			1	2		1		5		17	1	397
Butchers	7	436			18	2	9	4	32	8	5	8	23	9	79	2	4,194
Cabinetmakers	1	136			8			3	1	1	1	1	6	2	15		1,167
Carpenters and joiners	36	1,955		11	120	10	41	9	129	25	28	22	184	49	303	10	18,185
Clerks and accountants	33	896		122	85	7	25	10	129	35	20	31	120	11	112	5	11,345
Dressmakers	7	696			74		5	2	12	29	7	9	16	4	42	2	5,635
Engineers (locomotive, marine, and stationary)	5	261		5	24	1	3	2	13	10	1	18	32	4	17	2	2,143
Engravers		14					1		1			2	1		4		156
Furriers and fur workers		54						1	2			1	4		4		731
Gardeners	3	156		1	13	1	6	3	20	3	4	10	8	2	31	1	1,537
Hat and cap makers	2	103			6		1	1	3				1		5	1	923
Iron and steel workers	2	343			47		6		7	7	3	10	13	19	36		1,981
Jewelers		36		1	8				2	1		1	1		1		394
Locksmiths	7	554		3	16		1	1	57	5	4	5	5	10	53	1	3.407
Machinists	5	251		1	39		3	1	31	9	6	9	27	3	33	1	1,967

Mariners	46	454		18	58	3	14		61	9	2	28	385	17	85	2	8,737
Masons	9	1,661		6	75	3	13	8	63	31	60	12	53	71	135	12	11,779
Mechanics (not specified)	4	153		17	33		2	2	15	3		3	5	2	22		1,415
Metal workers (other than iron, steel, and tin)	1	86			30				9		1	3	6	2	6	1	999
Millers	2	176			4		1		12	3	1	1	5	2	34		1,064
Milliners	1	81		3	7			1	1	3		1			9		771
Miners	14	2,088			32	2	34	37	77	274	31	22	255	159	121	125	8,717
Painters and glaziers	5	375		1	36		6		16	13	3	11	23	4	38	4	4,531
Photographers	1	30		2	2		1		3	1		2	7		6		446
Plasterers	1	79			4		1	1			1	1	7	1	4		1,163
Plumbers	1	92		1	10	1			4	4	2	2	6	2	10	2	673
Printers	3	103		1	12		1		2	4	1	2	6		18		1,121
Saddlers and harnessmakers	2	79			3		3		9		2	1	6		8		745
Seamstresses	7	599		8	63		6	4	14	17	1	12	9	4	54		6,699
Shipwrights	1	42			2						1	1	1		1		155
Shoemakers	13	1,873		9	121	3	21	6	52	5	27	22	37	58	124	9	12,622
Stokers		44			1				1	1	1	2	10		6	1	729
Stonecutters	2	214			23		6	3	19	5	197	3	18	15	23		2,112
Tailors	18	2,834		5	165	1	9	27	48	13	15	24	65	25	189	5	26,982
Tanners and curriers	1	73			2		1		2						18		649
Textile workers (not specified)		78			70					11	6	1	2	1	3		889
Tinners	1	159		4	8		1	1	5		2	2	6	3	18		1,476
Tobacco workers		92			6			1	2		1	1	2		3		2,670
Upholsterers	1	42			1		1			2		1		1	4		425
Watch and clock makers	4	92			2		1	1	2	1		2	9		8		1,048
Weavers and spinners	10	454			250	10	4	1	12	21	13	3	14	2	28	2	3,481
Wheelwrights	1	91			3		3		5	4		4	4	1	20		559
Woodworkers (not specified)	1	97			6	1		1	12			1	3	1	9	1	765
Other skilled	11	360	1	11	69	1	6	2	23	14	11	11	47	8	48	4	3,786
Total	298	20,456	1	251	1,690	47	270	140	990	604	487	325	1,541	547	2,038	200	177,122
MISCELLANEOUS OCCUPATIONS.																	
Agents	5	50		15	7	1		10	33	1	1	3	6		4		881
Bankers	1	6		2	1			1	9			1	5		2		418
Draymen, hackmen, and teamsters	5	135			16		1	1	4	4	5		6	4	17	3	1,090
Farm laborers	319	67,802		42	1,372	10	415	147	1,814	395	512	391	752	3,306	3,442	181	239,125
Farmers	149	1,982	1	78	93	15	170	13	239	76	20	42	393	129	409	37	15,288
Fishermen	43	25		3	9		11	3			3		73	2	78	1	899
Hotel keepers	11	25		2	4	1			8	1			24		2	1	422
Laborers	629	47,033	1	34	2,051	38	554	207	569	674	583	316	3,413	2,150	3,908	315	226,345
Manufacturers	7	62		5	5	1			6	1	1	8	17		9		803
Merchants and dealers	104	1,022	2	235	98	9	9	45	203	16	10	49	255	26	113	4	17,054
Servants	250	17,310	1	55	1,475	19	467	40	320	208	227	71	705	290	1,740	83	115,984
Other miscellaneous	54	426		31	118	3	10	2	43	23	13	23	181	14	83	12	6,078
Total	1,577	135,878	5	502	5,249	97	1,637	469	3,248	1,399	1,375	904	5,830	5,921	9,807	637	624,387
No occupation (including women and children)	863	41,390	3	492	3,197	87	930	417	1,593	719	558	581	1,964	1,261	4,982	300	285,460
Grand total	2,786	198,681	11	1,483	10,215	235	2,852	1,040	5,945	2,751	2,436	1,845	9,482	7,741	16,966	1,152	1.100,735

Chart 5 shows each State's yearly proportion of the entire immigration to the United States, 1892 to 1906, and the proportions the several States bear to each other.

The uniformity of the proportion going to any one State year after year within certain limits is distinctive. Attention is invited to the fact that among the States that get the heavy immigration the proportions going to the States of New Jersey, Pennsylvania, and Ohio are gradually increasing, while the proportions going to New York and Massachusetts are on the decrease.

Chart 6 shows the character of the immigration to each State with regard to occupation during the past eight years. Eight of the principal classes are shown—i. e., laborers, servants, farm laborers, farmers, merchants, skilled (aliens skilled in the various trades), professional, and no occupation.

In view of the fact that the States having small immigration have as much color as those having heavy immigration, the total amount of color on chart representing each occupation should not be taken to indicate the proportion of aliens of that occupation for the whole country.

In Table X, as presented this year, a change has been made from the plan heretofore followed by consolidating the data so as to furnish the number and nationality of immigrants arrived in the United States from 1861 to 1906 by decades and fractions thereof instead of by years.

TABLE X.—IMMIGRATION BY DECADES, 1861–1906.

Country of last permanent residence.	1861-1870.		1871-1880.		1881-1890.	
	Number.	Per cent.	Number.	Per cent.	Number.	Per cent.
Austria-Hungary	7,794	0.33	72,969	2.6	353,722	6.7
Belgium	6,762	.28	7,221	.26	20,174	.38
Bulgaria, Servia, and Montenegro	....	....	....	....	....	....
Denmark	17,153	.72	31,771	1.1	88,132	1.7
France, including Corsica	38,293	1.6	72,201	2.6	50,463	.96
German Empire	821,214	35	718,182	25.5	1,452,970	28
Greece	....	....	....	....	2,053	.04
Italy, including Sicily and Sardinia	12,211	.51	55,702	2	307,310	5.9
Netherlands	9,278	.39	16,541	.6	53,701	1
Norway	45,679	1.9	95,323	3.4	176,586	3.4
Poland	....	....	....	....	34,973	.67
Portugal, including Cape Verde and Azore islands	1,854	.08	4,627	.16	11,917	.23
Roumania	....	....	....	....	5,938	.11
Russian Empire and Finland	4,650	.2	52,254	1.9	230,116	4.4
Spain, including Canary and Balearic islands	7,241	.3	5,266	.19	4,418	.08
Sweden	63,858	2.7	115,922	4	391,776	7.5
Switzerland	23,823	1	28,293	1	81,988	1.6
Turkey in Europe	....	....	....	....	1,185	.02
United Kingdom:						
England			437,706	15.6	644,680	12
Ireland	900,765	38	436,871	15.5	655,482	12
Scotland			87,564	3	149,869	2.9
Wales			6,631	.24	12,640	.24
Other Europe	172,712	7.3	16,800	.6	1,514	.03
Total Europe	2,142,287	90	2,261,904	80	4,731,607	90
China	65,202	2.7	123,200	4.4	61,711	1.2
Japan	(a)	....	(a)	....	(a)	....
India	(a)	....	(a)	....	(a)	....
Turkey in Asia	(a)	....	(a)	....	(a)	....
Other Asia	344	.01	603	.02	6,669	.13
Total Asia	65,546	2.8	123,803	4.4	68,380	1.3

TABLE X.—IMMIGRATION BY DECADES, 1861–1906—Continued.

Country of last permanent residence.	1861–1870.		1871–1880.		1881–1890.	
	Number.	Per cent.	Number.	Per cent.	Number.	Per cent.
Africa	321	0.01	239	0.01	764	0.015
Australia, Tasmania, and New Zealand	....	....	....	....	8,847	.17
British North America	139,000	5.8	383,269	14	392,802	7.5
Central America	99	.004	210	.01	462	.01
Mexico	2,278	.1	5,162	.18	1,913	.04
South America	1,494	.06	1,124	.04	2,304	.04
West Indies	9,842	.4	14,216	.5	29,042	.55
Other countries	16,412	.7	22,264	.8	10,492	.2
Grand total	2,377,279	....	2,812,191	....	5,246,613	....

Country of last permanent residence.	1891–1900.		1901–1905.		1906.	
	Number.	Per cent.	Number.	Per cent.	Number.	Per cent.
Austria-Hungary	592,707	16	944,239	25	265,138	24
Belgium	18,167	.5	16,884	.44	5,099	.46
Bulgaria, Servia, and Montenegro	160	.004	6,637	.17	4,666	.42
Denmark	50,231	1.4	33,968	.9	7,741	.7
France, including Corsica	30,770	.8	31,419	.8	9,386	.85
German Empire	505,152	14	176,995	4.6	37,564	3.4
Greece	15,979	.43	49,962	1.3	19,489	1.8
Italy, including Sicily and Sardinia	651,893	18	959,768	25	273,120	25
Netherlands	26,758	.73	18,501	.48	4,946	.45
Norway	95,014	2.6	103,065	2.7	21,730	2
Poland	96,721	2.6	....	....	....	....
Portugal, including Cape Verde and Azore Islands	27,323	.74	30,532	.8	8,517	.77
Roumania	12,750	.35	35,185	.92	4,476	.4
Russian Empire and Finland	505,290	14	658,735	17	215,665	20
Spain, including Canary and Balearic Islands	8,731	.24	10,243	.27	1,921	.17
Sweden	226,266	6	154,607	4	23,310	2
Switzerland	31,179	.85	17,820	.46	3,846	.35
Turkey in Europe	3,626	.1	10,909	.3	9,510	.86
United Kingdom:						
England	216,726	6	155,343	4	49,491	4.5
Ireland	388,416	10	184,096	4.8	34,995	3.2
Scotland	44,188	1.2	38,842	1	15,866	1.4
Wales	10,557	.3	6,972	.18	1,841	.17
Other Europe	189	.005	216	.006	48	.004
Total Europe	3,558,793	96.5	3,645,018	95	1,018,365	93
China	14,799	.4	12,792	.33	1,544	.14
Japan	24,806	.67	64,102	1.7	13,835	1.3
India	(a)	....	(a)	....	216	.02
Turkey in Asia	(a)	....	(a)	....	6,354	.58
Other Asia	31,631	.86	39,047	1	351	.03
Total Asia	71,236	1.9	115,941	3	22,300	2
Africa	350	.01	1,829	.05	712	.065
Australia, Tasmania, and New Zealand	2,198	.06	6,134	.16	1,682	.15
British North America	3,064	.08	7,239	.19	5,063	.46
Central America	569	.015	3,042	.08	1,060	.1
Mexico	971	.03	5,230	.14	1,997	.18
South America	1,075	.03	5,372	.14	2,757	.25
West Indies	33,066	.9	42,891	1.1	13,656	1.2
Other countries	16,242	.44	380	.01	33,143	3
Grand total	3,687,564	....	3,833,076	....	1,100,735	....

a Included with other Asia.

Tables XI to XIV, inclusive, correspond with those bearing similar numbers heretofore published, and will be found of value in the study of the problem of immigration in its various features.

TABLE XI.—IMMIGRANT ALIENS ADMITTED DURING THE CALENDAR YEAR 1905.

Country of last permanent residence.	Males.	Females.	Total.
Austria	82,191	36,811	119,002
Hungary	124,843	41,122	165,965
Belgium	3,181	1,528	4,709
Bulgaria, Servia, and Montenegro	2,533	62	2,595
Denmark	5,223	2,773	7,996
France, including Corsica	5,574	3,889	9,463
German Empire	21,586	15,357	36,943
Greece	14,517	633	15,150
Italy, including Sicily and Sardinia	216,268	51,273	267,541
Netherlands	3,082	1,758	4,840
Norway	15,038	8,164	23,202
Portugal, including Cape Verde and Azore Islands	4,178	2,763	6,941
Roumania	2,171	2,217	4,388
Russian Empire, and Finland	111,795	66,065	177,860
Spain, including Canary and Balearic Islands	1,914	404	2,318
Sweden	14,869	10,001	24,870
Switzerland	2,536	1,444	3,980
Turkey in Europe	6,639	194	6,833
United Kingdom:			
England	29,993	18,160	48,153
Ireland	18,754	18,890	37,644
Scotland	9,264	5,022	14,286
Wales	1,176	562	1,738
Other Europe	18	1	19
Total Europe	697,343	289,093	986,436
China	1,580	136	1,716
Japan	8,341	1,262	9,603
India	171	30	201
Turkey in Asia	4,931	1,961	6,892
Other Asia	3,005	282	3,287
Total Asia	18,028	3,671	21,699
Africa	489	127	616
Australia, Tasmania, and New Zealand	1,436	717	2,153
Pacific Islands, not specified	31	9	40
British North America	962	237	1,199
British Honduras	42	22	64
Other Central America	716	335	1,051
Mexico	2,102	446	2,548
South America	1,929	780	2,709
West Indies	12,065	2,951	15,016
United States	9,104	11,654	20,758
Other countries	102	51	153
Grand total	744,349	310,093	1,054,442

TABLE XII.—IMMIGRATION BY YEARS, 1820 TO 1906.

Period.	Number.	Period.	Number.
Year ending September 30—		Year ending June 30—continued.	
1820	8,385	1862	72,183
1821	9,127	1863	132,925
1822	6,911	1864	191,114
1823	6,354	1865	180,339
1824	7,912	1866	332,577
1825	10,199	1867	303,104
1826	10,837	1868	282,189
1827	18,875	1869	352,768
1828	27,382	1870	387,203
1829	22,520	1871	321,350
1830	23,322	1872	404,806
1831	22,633	1873	459,803
October 1, 1831, to December 31, 1832	60,482	1874	313,339
Year ending December 31—		1875	227,498
1833	58,640	1876	169,986
1834	65,365	1877	141,857
1835	45,374	1878	138,469
1836	76,242	1879	177,826
1837	79,340	1880	457,257
1838	38,914	1881	669,431
1839	68,069	1882	788,992
1840	84,066	1883	603,322
1841	80,289	1884	518,592
1842	104,565	1885	395,346
January 1 to September 30, 1843	52,496	1886	334,203
Year ending September 30—		1887	490,109
1844	78,615	1888	546,889
1845	114,371	1889	444,427
1846	154,416	1890	455,302
1847	234,968	1891	560,319
1848	226,527	1892	579,663
1849	297,024	1893	439,730
1850	310,004	1894	285,631
October 1 to December 31, 1850	59,976	1895	258,536
Year ending December 31—		1896	343,267
1851	379,466	1897	230,832
1852	371,603	1898	229,299
1853	368,645	1899	311,715
1854	427,833	1900	448,572
1855	200,877	1901	487,918
1856	195,857	1902	648,743
January 1 to June 30, 1857	112,123	1903	857,046
Year ending June 30—		1904	812,870
1858	191,942	1905	1,026,499
1859	129,571	1906	1,100,735
1860	133,143		
1861	142,877	Grand total	24,032,718

Chart 7 (old number 13) shows the wave of immigration into the United States from all countries since 1820. It is interesting to note the successive periodical increases, receding less each time, coincident with periods of financial depression, only to reach a greater height with the next ascending wave and passing the million mark in 1905, and ascending still higher in 1906. Thus the three periods of depression following 1857, 1873, and 1893 stand out prominently. This periodical rise and fall well represent the relative prosperity of the country, while the gradual average increase from decade to decade may be taken as an index of the country's development and growth and its capacity to employ larger quantities of the alien element.

TABLE XIII.—IMMIGRANT ALIENS ADMITTED INTO THE UNITED STATES, BY COUNTRIES, DURING THE SIX MONTHS ENDED DECEMBER 31, 1905.

Country of last permanent residence.	Males.	Females.	Total.
Austria	27,597	15,918	43,515
Hungary	37,255	17,881	55,136
Belgium	1,194	698	1,892
Bulgaria, Servia, and Montenegro	1,266	41	1,307
Denmark	1,739	1,304	3,043
France, including Corsica	3,247	2,409	5,656
German Empire	10,258	8,155	18,413
Greece	6,909	370	7,279
Italy, including Sicily and Sardinia	61,817	27,494	89,311
Netherlands	975	649	1,624
Norway	4,378	3,939	8,317
Portugal, including Cape Verde and Azore Islands	1,986	1,615	3,601
Roumania	1,182	1,281	2,463
Russian Empire, and Finland	42,239	36,915	79,154
Spain, including Canary and Balearic Islands	773	210	983
Sweden	6,106	5,466	11,572
Switzerland	1,048	733	1,781
Turkey in Europe	3,134	149	3,283
United Kingdom—			
England	14,525	10,070	24,595
Ireland	6,691	8,117	14,808
Scotland	3,876	2,672	6,548
Wales	549	279	828
Other Europe	12	....	12
Total Europe	238,756	146,365	385,121
China	964	83	1,047
Japan	3,736	690	4,426
India	73	12	85
Turkey in Asia	2,927	1,207	4,134
Other Asia	175	31	206
Total Asia	7,875	2,023	9,898
Africa	216	71	287
Australia, Tasmania, and New Zealand	630	291	921
Pacific Islands, not specified	19	4	23
British North America	597	140	737
British Honduras	8	3	11
Other Central America	312	136	448
Mexico	934	208	1,142
South America	975	421	1,396
West Indies	6,261	216	6,477
United States	9,104	11,654	20,758
Other countries	56	21	77
Grand total	265,743	161,553	427,296

TABLE XIV.—IMMIGRANT ALIENS ADMITTED INTO THE UNITED STATES, BY COUNTRIES, DURING THE SIX MONTHS ENDED JUNE 30, 1906.

Country of last permanent residence.	Males.	Females.	Total.
Austria	48,378	19,705	68,083
Hungary	76,214	22,190	98,404
Belgium	2,326	881	3,207
Bulgaria, Servia, and Montenegro	3,295	64	3,359
Denmark	3,329	1,369	4,698
France, including Corsica	2,344	1,386	3,730
German Empire	11,489	7,662	19,151
Greece	11,654	556	12,210
Italy, including Sicily and Sardinia	154,298	29,511	183,809
Netherlands	2,067	1,255	3,322
Norway	9,753	3,660	13,413
Portugal, including Cape Verde and Azore Islands	3,026	1,890	4,916
Roumania	1,116	897	2,013
Russian Empire, and Finland	85,014	51,497	136,511
Spain, including Canary and Balearic Islands	798	140	938
Sweden	7,729	4,009	11,738
Switzerland	1,412	653	2,065
Turkey in Europe	5,996	231	6,227
United Kingdom—			
England	16,458	8,438	24,896
Ireland	11,543	8,644	20,187
Scotland	6,624	2,694	9,318
Wales	756	257	1,013
Other Europe	23	13	36
Total Europe	465,642	167,602	633,244
China	440	57	497
Japan	8,608	801	9,409
India	114	17	131
Turkey in Asia	1,611	609	2,220
Other Asia	131	14	145
Total Asia	10,904	1,498	12,402
Africa	346	79	425
Australia, Tasmania, and New Zealand	535	226	761
Pacific Islands, not specified	9	5	14
British North America	3,789	537	4,326
British Honduras	35	34	69
Other Central America	483	129	612
Mexico	709	146	855
South America	967	394	1,361
West Indies	4,840	2,339	7,179
United States	10,417	1,722	12,139
Other countries	44	8	52
Grand total	498,720	174,719	673,439

Table XV shows the number of "nonimmigrant" aliens admitted during the year. It includes all aliens admitted who avowed an intention not to settle in the United States, and all returning to resume domicils formerly acquired in this country. By selecting any one of the countries of last permanent residence shown in the first column thereof and following across the page, one can determine at a glance how many persons have come from such country to the United States with the intention of proceeding to any of the other countries represented. For instance, we find thus that 2,494 persons entered the United States from the United Kingdom with the intention of returning thereto, and that 8,860 entered therefrom with the intention of proceeding to British North America; that our country was visited by 1,541 Italians, 376 Germans, and 323 French, whose intention it was to return to their respective native countries; and that 20,616 aliens gave both their last place of permanent residence and their destination as the United States—these being those returning from visits to their former homes.

TABLE XV.—NONIMMIGRANT ALIENS ADMITTED INTO THE UNITED STATES DURING THE FISCAL YEAR ENDED JUNE 30, 1906, BY COUNTRIES OF LAST PERMANENT RESIDENCE AND COUNTRIES OF FINAL DESTINATION.

Countries of last permanent residence.	Austria-Hungary.	Belgium.	Bulgaria, Servia, and Montenegro.	Denmark.	France, including Corsica.	German Empire.	Greece.	Italy, including Sicily and Sardinia.	Netherlands.	Norway.	Portugal, including Cape Verde and Azore islands.	Roumania.	Russian Empire.	Spain, including Canary and Balearic Islands.	Sweden.	Switzerland.	Turkey in Europe.	United Kingdom.	Other Europe.	Total Europe.
Austria-Hungary	172					1							1					6		180
Belgium		70			1	1								2				1		75
Bulgaria, Servia, and Montenegro		1																		1
Denmark				14																14
France, including Corsica			1		323				2									5		331
German Empire	3				1	376								2				2		384
Greece	1						32													33
Italy, including Sicily and Sardinia					3			1,541										3		1,547
Netherlands								1	36	1								1		39
Norway						1				41								1		43
Portugal, including Cape Verde and Azore Islands											9									9
Roumania												1								1
Russian Empire					8	9			1				84		1			9		112
Spain, including Canary and Balearic Islands					9			1						24	3	1		5		43
Sweden															87	1		2		90
Switzerland					4											24				28
Turkey in Europe																	9	3		12
United Kingdom	2	1			5			1										2,494		2,503
Other Europe																			1	1
Total Europe	178	72	1	14	354	388	32	1,544	39	42	9	1	85	28	91	26	9	2,532	1	5,446
China		3			24	48		2	3	2	5		19		2	2		242	2	354
Japan		3			19	29				2			2	1		2	1	238	2	299
India						5			2									40		47
Turkey in Asia		1			4													1		6
Other Asia					1	2			2				3					5		13
Total Asia		7			48	84		2	7	4	5		24	1	2	4	1	526	4	719
Africa					1									1				14		16
Australia, Tasmania, and New Zealand		1			2	10		1	1									478		493
Pacific islands, not specified	1				43	2			5									8		59
British North America	62	14	1		33	14	5	83	3	7			22		3	2	4	199		452

British Honduras					1	3												18		22
Other Central America	3	8		2	96	111	5	17		2			1	20	1	3		100	9	378
Mexico	17	7			174	88		100	2	2			1	192	5	7	13	197	1	806
South America	8	3		2	144	90		33	8		1			5		10	1	154	2	461
West Indies	11	11		15	329	131		97	9	22	18		2	307	3	4	1	624	3	1,587
United States	2				4	2	1	4										36		49
Other countries																		1		1
Grand total	282	123	2	33	1,229	923	43	1,881	74	79	33	1	135	554	105	56	29	4,887	20	10,489
Male	239	100	2	28	881	720	40	1,800	62	66	18	1	113	419	97	46	25	3,737	17	8,411
Female	43	23		5	348	203	3	81	12	13	15		22	135	8	10	4	1,150	3	2,078

Countries of last permanent residence.	China.	Japan.	India.	Turkey in Asia.	Other Asia.	Total Asia.	Africa.	Australia, Tasmania, and New Zealand.	Pacific islands, not specified.	British North America.	British Honduras.	Other Central America.	Mexico.	South America.	West Indies.	United States.	Other countries.	Grand total.	Male.	Female.
Austria-Hungary		5			1	6		11		2,316		6	21	2	8		13	2,563	1,999	564
Belgium	2	1				3			5	195		14	7	3	21		7	330	269	61
Bulgaria, Servia, and Montenegro										24			2		2			29	24	5
Denmark	2					2				87		2	4		4		3	116	82	34
France, including Corsica	7	15			1	23		8	20	741	8	83	298	63	298		54	1,927	1,318	609
German Empire	13	23			1	37		5	13	435	2	153	159	46	74		80	1,388	1,041	347
Greece										164			4	1			4	206	198	8
Italy, including Sicily and Sardinia		3				3		3		5,390		32	157	11	46		116	7,305	6,634	671
Netherlands	2					2		1		130		12	3	1	15		13	216	176	40
Norway							11			210		17	3	2	28		8	322	257	65
Portugal, including Cape Verde and Azore islands										4			2		9		470	494	391	103
Roumania										53			1					55	33	22
Russian Empire		2				2				1,889			2	1	6		16	2,028	1,225	803
Spain, including Canary and Balearic islands	1					1				9	1	17	338	7	492		29	937	718	219
Sweden	1	1				2			1	231			5		1		26	356	275	81
Switzerland		1				1		1		81		9	15	4	3		19	161	112	49
Turkey in Europe					2	2				321			12				56	403	358	45
United Kingdom	112	181	5		1	299	2	290	12	8,860	22	39	274	62	332	5	660	13,360	9,807	3,553
Other Europe										1					1			3	3	
Total Europe	140	232	5		6	383	13	319	51	21,141	33	384	1,307	203	1,340	5	1,574	32,199	24,920	7,279
China	34	1				35				16		1	34	1	200		14	655	551	104
Japan		69				69		3		17			95	4	1		23	511	436	75
India			10			10			5	18							2	82	60	22

TABLE XV.—NONIMMIGRANT ALIENS ADMITTED INTO THE UNITED STATES DURING THE FISCAL YEAR ENDED JUNE 30, 1906, BY COUNTRIES OF LAST PERMANENT RESIDENCE AND COUNTRIES OF FINAL DESTINATION—Continued.

Countries of last permanent residence.	China.	Japan.	India.	Turkey in Asia.	Other Asia.	Total Asia.	Africa.	Australia, Tasmania, and New Zealand.	Pacific islands, not specified.	British North America.	British Honduras.	Other Central America.	Mexico.	South America.	West Indies.	United States.	Other countries.	Grand total.	Male.	Female.
Turkey in Asia				36		36				195			2		5		2	246	185	61
Other Asia					5	5				7							1	26	22	4
Total Asia	34	70	10	36	5	155		3	5	253		1	131	5	206		42	1,520	1,254	266
Africa	1	2				3	6			51			26				4	106	76	30
Australia, Tasmania, and New Zealand	2	1				3		206	6	93		1	6	2	1		27	838	538	300
Pacific islands, not specified	1					1			15	7				2			7	91	63	28
British North America		8		27		35	1	3	3	2,279			6	1	12		165	2,957	2,018	939
British Honduras											15	4			5		5	51	40	11
Other Central America	53	4		5		62		1		23	10	261	14	5	21		49	824	632	192
Mexico	58	8		34	4	104				68	3	7	449	22	4		133	1,596	1,195	401
South America		2	1	6		9		1	1	64		1	23	194	51		82	887	663	224
West Indies	200	2	2	3	5	212	5	3		743		19	5	16	729	252	197	3,768	2,683	1,085
United States	1	2				3				95	1	1	3	2	4	20,616	2	20,776	17,423	3,353
Other countries														1	3			5	5	
Grand total	490	331	18	111	20	970	25	536	81	24,817	62	679	1,970	453	2,376	20,873	2,287	65,618		
Male	439	264	16	90	14	823	18	368	61	18,644	45	506	1,486	353	1,776	17,256	1,762		51,510	
Female	51	67	2	21	6	147	7	168	20	6,173	17	173	484	100	600	3,617	524			14,108

Table XVI, giving the inward passenger movement for the year, is also an addition to the report. It furnishes, as nearly as bare figures can, an idea of the work performed at the different ports, covering not only the number of immigrant and nonimmigrant aliens that arrived, but also the number rejected at each port, and the number of American citizens returning to their homes through such ports.

TABLE XVI.—INWARD PASSENGER MOVEMENT, FISCAL YEAR ENDED JUNE 30, 1906.

Port.	Immigrant aliens admitted.	Nonimmigrant aliens admitted.	United States citizens arrived.	Aliens debarred.	Grand total.
New York, N. Y	880,046	44,975	135,959	7,877	1,068,847
Boston, Mass	62,229	5,103	12,285	664	80,281
Baltimore, Md	54,064	290	1,367	301	56,022
Philadelphia, Pa	23,186	577	3,924	152	27,839
San Francisco, Cal	4,138	1,767	4,641	165	10,711
San Juan, P. R	1,452	428	1,442	5	3,327
Bangor, Me	10				10
Brownsville, Tex	55	4		6	65
Brunswick, Ga	11				11
Douglas, Ariz	16		1,396		1,412
Eagle Pass, Tex	140	230		29	399
El Paso, Tex	1,668	256		182	2,106
Fernandina, Fla	3				3
Galveston, Tex	6,201	50	340	47	6,638
Gulfport, Miss	21			2	23
Honolulu, Hawaii	9,380	177	313	80	9,950
Jacksonville, Fla	20	9	5	1	35
Ketchikan, Alaska	73	2			75
Key West, Fla	5,319	965	8,356	63	14,703
Laredo, Tex	671	314		224	1,209
Miami, Fla	599	54	2,158	2	2,813
Mobile, Ala	292	166	1,950		2,408
Naco, Ariz	190	63		13	266
New Bedford, Mass	1,994	471	249	10	2,724
New Orleans, La	2,051	513	2,401	33	4,998
Nogales, Ariz	32	42		14	88
Norfolk, Va	56	33	43	2	134
Pensacola, Fla	56		2	1	59
Portland, Me	814	2,728	12	14	3,568
Providence, R. I	19	28	2		49
Savannah, Ga	26			1	27
Seattle, Wash	1,916	347	643	95	3,001
Total through United States ports	1,056,738	59,592	177,488	9,983	1,303,801
Through Canada	43,997	6,026		2,449	52,472
Grand total	1,100,735	65,618	177,488	12,432	1,356,273
Males	764,463	51,510	101,563	10,213	927,749
Females	336,272	14,108	75,925	2,219	428,524

Table XVII, giving the outward passenger movement for the fiscal year ended June 30, 1906, heretofore published by the Bureau of Statistics of this Department, is inserted in this report at this point with a view to making the statistics as complete as possible. Attention is directed to the note inserted immediately under the caption of the table, in order that no misunderstanding may occur as to its scope and significance.

TABLE XVII.—PASSENGERS DEPARTED FROM SEAPORTS OF THE UNITED STATES FOR FOREIGN COUNTRIES, OTHER THAN BRITISH NORTH AMERICA, DURING THE FISCAL YEAR ENDED JUNE 30, 1906.

[In the absence of law requiring masters of vessels departing from the United States for foreign countries to deliver to collectors of customs returns of the passengers embarking on such vessels, reliance is had upon the courtesy of the agents of steamship and packet lines for information on the outward passenger movement. The following statistics relate only to the departure from the seaports indicated in the table, and comprise only the data secured in the manner above indicated, but it is probable that the departures given embrace nearly the entire passenger movement from the United States to foreign countries from our seaports.]

Line of vessels.	Ports of departure and destination.	Cabin passengers.							Passengers other than cabin.							Total passengers departed.
		Under 12 years of age.			12 years of age and over.			Total cabin.	Under 12 years of age.			12 years of age and over.			Total other than cabin.	
		Males.	Females.	Total.	Males.	Females.	Total.		Males.	Females.	Total.	Males.	Females.	Total.		
	From Baltimore, Md.:															
Atlantic Fruit Co.	Port Antonio, Jamaica				40	16	56	56								56
Di Giorgis Importing and Steamship Co.	Honduras				2	3	5	5								5
North German Lloyd	Bremen, Germany	85	74	159	667	823	1,490	1,649	134	110	244	1,151	616	1,767	2,011	3,660
United Fruit Co.	Port Antonio, Jamaica				87	75	162	162								162
	Banes, Cuba	2	2	4	9	8	17	21								21
Sailing vessels	Colombia				2		2	2								2
	Total, Baltimore, Md.	87	76	163	807	925	1,732	1,895	134	110	244	1,151	616	1,767	2,011	3,906
	From Bangor, Me.:															
British steamship	Scotland		1	1		1	1	2								2
Sailing vessel	Nova Scotia					1	1	1								1
	Total, Bangor, Me.		1	1		2	2	3								3
	From Boston, Mass.:															
Cunard	Liverpool, England	158	115	273	1,874	2,195	4,069	4,342	557	537	1,094	4,128	2,953	7,081	8,175	12,517
White Star	Do	72	81	153	1,367	1,292	2,659	2,812	295	254	549	1,891	1,545	3,436	3,985	6,797
	Mediterranean ports	51	44	95	907	1,492	2,399	2,494	474	488	962	2,810	4,444	7,254	8,216	10,710
Leyland	Liverpool, England	24	14	38	280	453	733	771								771
Allan	Glasgow, Scotland	6	6	12	104	156	260	272	10	10	20	35	33	68	88	360
United Fruit Co.	Port Antonio, Jamaica	18	9	27	679	416	1,095	1,122								1,122
	Port Limon, Costa Rica		1	1	38	24	62	63								63
	Total, Boston, Mass.	329	270	599	5,249	6,028	11,277	11,876	1,336	1,289	2,625	8,864	8,975	17,839	20,464	32,340

	From New Bedford, Mass.:														
Insular Navigation Co.	Azores								20	25	45	141	84	225	270	270
Sailing vessel	Cape Verde Islands								3	9	12	145	23	168	180	180
	Total, New Bedford, Mass.								23	34	57	286	107	393	450	450
	From New York, N. Y.:															
Allan State	Glasgow, Scotland	13	15	28	145	243	388	416	13	9	22	45	30	75	97	513
American	Southampton, England	357	126	483	5,073	1,778	6,851	7,334	668	244	912	7,535	2,829	10,364	11,276	18,610
Anchor	Glasgow, Scotland	364	313	677	4,106	2,754	6,860	7,537	458	368	826	5,448	2,502	7,950	8,776	16,313
	Mediterranean ports	2	1	3	42	40	82	85	168	153	321	3,335	841	4,176	4,497	4,582
Atlantic Transport Co.	London, England	94	62	156	1,956	1,277	3,233	3,389								3,389
Booth	British West Indies	10	16	26	73	82	155	181	2	6	8	45	20	65	73	254
	Brazil	5	3	8	52	14	66	74				15	3	18	18	92
	Peru				6	2	8	8								8
Clyde	West Indies	16	14	30	309	106	415	445								445
Cunard	Queenstown and Liverpool, England.	667	398	1,065	9,001	6,579	15,580	16,645	1,079	856	1,935	8,997	6,155	15,152	17,087	33,732
	Mediterranean ports	53	74	127	761	1,249	2,010	2,137	288	286	574	3,609	3,016	6,625	7,199	9,336
Fabre	Italy	12	6	18	116	62	178	196	592	87	679	7,231	521	7,752	8,431	8,627
French	France	201	134	335	5,427	3,915	9,342	9,677	891	593	1,484	15,294	6,697	21,991	23,475	33,152
Hamburg-American: Atlas service	Central America and West Indies.	60	43	103	1,301	617	1,918	2,021								2,021
Regular and express service	Plymouth, Cherbourg, and Hamburg.	950	640	1,590	11,208	6,368	17,576	19,166	1,663	995	2,658	13,213	6,353	19,566	22,224	41,390
	Naples and Genoa, Italy	97	62	159	1,800	1,313	3,113	3,272	273	179	452	4,377	2,050	6,427	6,879	10,151
Holland-American	Rotterdam, Netherlands	317	370	687	2,923	3,401	6,324	7,011	740	850	1,590	10,470	4,180	14,650	16,240	23,251
Italian	Mediterranean ports	70	50	120	696	232	928	1,048	418	163	581	5,720	681	6,401	6,982	8,030
	Bombay, India											2		2	2	2
	Alexandria, Egypt				1		1	1					1	1	1	2
	Montevideo, Uruguay											1		1	1	1
Lamport & Holt	South America	21	32	53	323	139	462	515	54	50	104	333	93	426	530	1,045
La Veloce	Mediterranean ports	28	26	54	200	177	377	431	191	100	291	3,717	557	4,274	4,565	4,996
Munson	West Indies	238	151	389	234	131	365	754								754
North German Lloyd	Bremen, Germany	1,308	768	2,076	14,237	7,323	21,560	23,636	2,733	1,627	4,360	18,333	7,073	25,406	29,766	53,402
	Genoa, Italy	286	141	427	3,723	1,817	5,540	5,967	627	369	996	7,169	2,989	10,158	11,154	17,121
New York and Porto Rico	Porto Rico	80	63	143	1,131	863	1,994	2,137	3	2	5	74	14	88	93	2,230
Panama Railroad	Colon, Panama	171	133	304	3,880	911	4,791	5,095	15	18	33	470	76	546	579	5,674
Quebec	Bermuda and West Indies.	78	75	153	2,352	2,187	4,539	4,692	24	26	50	496	383	879	929	5,621
Red D	San Juan, P. R.	46	36	82	782	289	1,071	1,153								1,153
	Curaçao, Dutch West Indies.	3		3	58	20	78	81								81
	Venezuela	11	6	17	170	59	229	246								246
Red Star	Antwerp, Belgium	587	203	790	5,480	1,875	7,355	8,145	1,246	457	1,703	11,647	4,258	15,905	17,608	25,753
Royal Dutch West Indian Mail.	West Indies and South America.	2	4	6	104	32	136	142								142
Royal Mail Steam Packet	Cherbourg and Southampton, England.	1	3	4	20	26	46	50								50
	West Indies and South America.	25	26	51	722	534	1,256	1,307				16	2	18	18	1,325

TABLE XVII.—PASSENGERS DEPARTED FROM SEAPORTS OF THE UNITED STATES FOR FOREIGN COUNTRIES, OTHER THAN BRITISH NORTH AMERICA, DURING THE FISCAL YEAR ENDED JUNE 30, 1906—Continued.

Line of vessels.	Ports of departure and destination.	Cabin passengers.							Passengers other than cabin.							Total passengers departed.
		Under 12 years of age.			12 years of age and over.			Total cabin.	Under 12 years of age.			12 years of age and over.			Total other than cabin.	
		Males.	Females.	Total.	Males.	Females.	Total.		Males.	Females.	Total.	Males.	Females.	Total.		
	From New York, N. Y.—Con.															
Scandinavian-American	Denmark	85	109	194	608	764	1,372	1,566	119	145	264	1,070	600	1,670	1,934	3,500
	Norway	57	55	112	368	476	844	956	178	177	355	1,800	992	2,792	3,147	4,103
	Sweden	3	4	7	14	12	26	33	152	136	288	716	770	1,486	1,774	1,807
Spanish steamship	Mediterranean ports	27	18	45	187	97	284	329	126	101	227	2,906	235	3,141	3,368	3,697
	West Indies	21	17	38	111	54	165	203								203
Trinidad	Trinidad and other West Indian ports.	12	9	21	154	68	222	243								243
Ward	West Indies and Mexico	306	203	509	6,373	1,490	7,863	8,372	229	140	369	3,200	692	3,892	4,261	12,633
White Star	Liverpool, England	480	286	766	11,618	5,104	16,722	17,488	868	551	1,419	11,418	5,554	16,972	18,391	35,879
	Naples, Italy	71	28	99	2,393	1,090	3,483	3,582	346	177	523	5,544	2,262	7,806	8,329	11,911
Wilson	Hull, England	5	4	9	26	42	68	77								77
	Total New York	7,240	4,727	11,967	100,264	55,612	155,876	167,843	14,164	8,865	23,029	154,246	62,429	216,675	239,704	407,547
	From Philadelphia, Pa.:															
American	Liverpool, England	113	116	229	1,066	1,603	2,669	2,898	256	250	506	2,474	984	3,458	3,964	6,862
Allan	Glasgow, Scotland				31	14	45	45								45
	St. Johns, Newfoundland	3	5	8	28	13	41	49								49
Hamburg-American	Hamburg, Germany				1		1	1								1
Red Star	Antwerp, Belgium	4	6	10	76	219	295	305								305
United Fruit Co	West Indian ports	9	3	12	494	377	871	883								883
	Total Philadelphia, Pa.	129	130	259	1,696	2,226	3,922	4,181	256	250	506	2,474	984	3,458	3,964	8,145
	From Portland, Me.:															
Dominion	Liverpool, England				30	18	48	48								48
	From Porto Rico:															
Compañía Transatlántica Española.	Mediterranean ports and West Indies.	53	44	97	286	151	437	534	50	59	109	326	125	451	560	1,094
Compagnie Générale Transatlantique.	France and West Indies	39	25	64	188	83	271	335	58	57	115	382	200	582	697	1,032
Red D	West Indies and South America.	9	2	11	115	47	162	173	4		4	117	37	154	158	331

Empresa de Vapores	West Indies	20	24	44	226	144	370	414	67	63	130	373	172	545	675	1,089
Hamburg-American	Hamburg, Germany	1	4	5	3	6	9	14								14
Norwegian	Cuba	5	1	6	7	4	11	17				2	4	6	6	23
Royal Mail	West Indies				4	1	5	5								5
La Veloce	Mediterranean ports				3	3	6	6								6
Vapor Dominicano	West Indies				7	4	11	11				5	1	6	6	17
Vapores Española	Mediterranean ports	7	6	13	27	8	35	48				12	4	16	16	64
Norton	Cuba				1		1	1								1
	Total Porto Rico	134	106	240	867	451	1,318	1,558	179	179	358	1,217	543	1,760	2,118	3,676
	From Providence, R. I.:															
Sailing vessel	Africa									5	5	44	9	53	58	58
	From Galveston, Tex.:															
North German Lloyd	Bremen, Germany	40	52	92	258	257	515	607	25	27	52	231	87	318	370	977
Gulf Transport	Liverpool, England	7	4	11	15	13	28	39								39
Leyland	Do	5	8	13	15	20	35	48								48
Head	Belfast, Ireland				1	1	2	2								2
	Total Galveston, Tex	52	64	116	289	291	580	696	25	27	52	231	87	318	370	1,066
	From Key West, Fla.:															
P. and O	Nassau and Habana	395	317	712	8,868	4,805	13,673	14,385								14,385
McKay	Cuba	123	101	224	752	350	1,102	1,326								1,326
Sailing vessels	Central America and West Indies	18	23	41	207	129	336	377								377
	Total Key West, Fla.:	536	441	977	9,827	5,284	15,111	16,088								16,088
	Mobile, Ala.:															
Munson	Cuba				1,033	559	1,592	1,592								1,592
Orr and Laubenheimer Co	Belize, British Honduras				19	3	22	22								22
United Fruit Co	Central America				13	3	16	16								16
Bluefields	Bluefields, Nicaragua				26	9	35	35								35
Central American Steamship Line.	Central America				23		23	23								23
Camors, McConnell Co	Bocas del Toro, Panama				7	1	8	8								8
	Total Mobile, Ala				1,121	575	1,696	1,696								1,696
	From New Orleans, La.:															
Bluefields	Bluefields, Nicaragua	9	3	12	113	30	143	155				20	2	22	22	177
Celfalu Brothers	Puerto Cortez, Honduras				12	3	15	15								15
Independent	Ceiba, Honduras	11	11	22	125	40	165	187								187
Leyland	London, Liverpool, and Havre.	17	15	32	91	115	206	238				2	2	4	4	242
Head	Belfast, Ireland	2	3	5	3	1	4	9								9
Morgan	Cuba	21	23	44	841	396	1,237	1,281								1,281
United Fruit Co	Central America	41	24	65	676	184	860	925	1		1	48	4	52	53	978
Central America	Do				2		2	2								2

TABLE XVII.—PASSENGERS DEPARTED FROM SEAPORTS OF THE UNITED STATES FOR FOREIGN COUNTRIES, OTHER THAN BRITISH NORTH AMERICA, DURING THE FISCAL YEAR ENDED JUNE 30, 1906—Continued.

Line of vessels.	Ports of departure and destination.	Cabin passengers.							Passengers other than cabin.							Total passengers departed.
		Under 12 years of age.			12 years of age and over.			Total cabin.	Under 12 years of age.			12 years of age and over.			Total other than cabin.	
		Males.	Females.	Total.	Males.	Females.	Total.		Males.	Females.	Total.	Males.	Females.	Total.		
	From New Orleans, La.—Con.															
Texas Transportation and Terminal Co.	Havre, France	2	2	4	15	17	32	36				12	4	16	16	52
	Palermo, Italy								57	41	98	205	61	266	364	364
Planters	Central America	2		2	5	3	8	10								10
Navigazione General Italiano.	Palermo, Italy	1	2	3	14	10	24	27	39	28	67	194	62	256	323	350
	Total New Orleans, La.	106	83	189	1,897	799	2,696	2,885	97	69	166	481	135	616	782	3,667
	From Hawaii:															
Oceanic	Australian ports	3		3	34	26	60	63				2		2	2	65
Canadian and Australian	Do.				17	3	20	20				8	5	13	13	33
Occidental and Oriental	Hongkong, Manila, China, and Japan.	1		1	14	5	19	20	83	74	157	467	115	582	739	759
Pacific Mail	Do.	11	11	22	102	87	189	211	268	224	492	1,257	319	1,576	2,068	2,279
Toyo Kisen Kaisha	Hongkong and Japan		1	1	3	7	10	11	22	17	39	69	24	93	132	143
	Total Hawaii	15	12	27	170	128	298	325	373	315	688	1,803	463	2,266	2,954	3,279
	From Puget Sound, Wash.:															
Boston	Hongkong, Manila, China, and Japan.	7	16	23	110	91	201	224				182	3	185	185	409
Nippon Yusen Kaisha	Do.	1	1	2	83	22	105	107	4		4	573	30	603	607	714
Great Northern	Do.	10	15	25	357	236	593	618		1	1	410	7	417	418	1,036
Oceanic	Hongkong and Japan											34		34	34	34
Alfred Hoyt, Liverpool Line.	Hongkong											6		6	6	6
	Total Puget Sound, Wash.	18	32	50	550	349	899	949	4	1	5	1,205	40	1,245	1,250	2,199
	From San Francisco, Cal.:															
Oceanic	Auckland, Sidney, and Society Islands.	66	50	116	734	518	1,252	1,368				173	12	185	185	1,553

Oriental	Hongkong, Shanghai, and Japan.	2	3	5	114	68	182	187				437	6	443	443	630
	China (Chinese)											624		624	624	624
Occidental and Oriental	Hongkong, China, and Japan.				143	99	242	242				207	3	210	210	452
	China (Chinese)											818		818	818	818
Kosmos	Central and South America.				42	29	71	71				3		3	3	74
Pacific Mail	Hongkong and Shanghai	56	43	99	670	575	1,245	1,344				43	20	63	63	1,407
	China (Chinese)											4,359		4,359	4,359	4,359
	Japan	28	22	50	437	370	807	857				1,093	21	1,114	1,114	1,971
	Central and South America.				433	124	557	557				110	14	124	124	681
	Total San Francisco, Cal.	152	118	270	2,573	1,783	4,356	4,626				7,867	76	7,943	7,943	12,569
	Grand total	8,798	6,060	14,858	125,340	74,471	199,811	214,669	16,591	11,144	27,735	179,869	74,464	254,333	282,068	496,737

RECAPITULATION.

Classification.	Cabin passengers.							Passengers other than cabin.							Total passengers departed.
	Under 12 years of age.			12 years of age and over.			Total cabin.	Under 12 years of age.			12 years of age and over.			Total other than cabin.	
	Males.	Females.	Total.	Males.	Females.	Total.		Males.	Females.	Total.	Males.	Females.	Total.		
PORT OF DEPARTURE.															
Baltimore, Md	87	76	163	807	925	1,732	1,895	134	110	244	1,151	616	1,767	2,011	3,906
Bangor, Me		1	1		2	2	3								3
Boston, Mass	329	270	599	5,249	6,028	11,277	11,876	1,336	1,289	2,625	8,864	8,975	17,839	20,464	32,340
New Bedford, Mass								23	34	57	286	107	393	450	450
New York, N. Y	7,240	4,727	11,967	100,264	55,612	155,876	167,843	14,164	8,865	23,029	154,246	62,429	216,675	239,704	407,547
Philadelphia, Pa	129	130	259	1,696	2,226	3,922	4,181	256	250	506	2,474	984	3,458	3,964	8,145
Portland, Me				30	18	48	48								48
Porto Rico	134	106	240	867	451	1,318	1,558	179	179	358	1,217	543	1,760	2,118	3,676
Providence, R. I									5	5	44	9	53	58	58
Galveston, Tex	52	64	116	289	291	580	696	25	27	52	231	87	318	370	1,066
Key West, Fla	536	441	977	9,827	5,284	15,111	16,088								16,088
Mobile, Ala				1,121	575	1,696	1,696								1,696
New Orleans, La	106	83	189	1,897	799	2,696	2,885	97	69	166	481	135	616	782	3,667
Hawaii	15	12	27	170	128	298	325	373	315	688	1,803	463	2,266	2,954	3,279

TABLE XVII.—PASSENGERS DEPARTED FROM SEAPORTS OF THE UNITED STATES FOR FOREIGN COUNTRIES, OTHER THAN BRITISH NORTH AMERICA, DURING THE FISCAL YEAR ENDED JUNE 30, 1906—Continued.

RECAPITULATION—Continued.

Classification.	Cabin passengers.							Passengers other than cabin.							Total passengers departed.
	Under 12 years of age.			12 years of age and over.			Total cabin.	Under 12 years of age.			12 years of age and over.			Total other than cabin.	
	Males.	Females.	Total.	Males.	Females.	Total.		Males.	Females.	Total.	Males.	Females.	Total.		
PORT OF DEPARTURE—continued.															
Puget Sound, Wash	18	32	50	550	349	899	949	4	1	5	1,205	40	1,245	1,250	2,199
San Francisco, Cal	152	118	270	2,573	1,783	4,356	4,626	....	....	....	7,867	76	7,943	7,943	12,569
Shipped by—															
Steamers	8,780	6,037	14,817	125,131	74,341	199,472	214,289	16,588	11,130	27,718	179,680	74,432	254,112	281,830	496,119
Sailing vessels	18	23	41	209	130	339	380	3	14	17	189	32	221	238	618
Chinese departed	....	....	....	....	....	....	....	....	....	....	5,801	....	5,801	5,801	5,801
TOTAL PASSENGERS DEPARTED.															
1890	5,297	4,099	9,396	66,120	30,359	96,489	105,885	8,698	7,532	16,230	83,110	32,914	116,024	132,254	238,139
1891	5,604	3,756	9,360	65,056	32,692	97,748	107,108	9,268	6,004	15,272	89,034	35,092	124,126	139,398	246,506
1892	5,717	3,706	9,423	61,763	33,966	95,729	105,152	9,999	5,969	15,968	96,834	38,602	135,436	151,404	256,556
1893	5,503	3,727	9,230	57,904	27,995	85,899	95,129	8,352	5,444	13,796	88,315	33,384	121,699	135,495	230,664
1894	7,622	4,834	12,456	70,864	38,611	109,475	121,931	15,798	9,307	25,105	112,941	52,794	165,735	190,840	312,771
1895	5,828	3,812	9,640	64,887	38,366	103,253	112,893	17,257	10,612	27,869	123,845	64,951	188,796	216,665	329,558
1898 [a]	5,111	3,780	8,891	54,533	31,130	85,663	94,554	10,001	5,789	15,790	78,621	36,446	115,067	130,857	225,411
1899	6,418	4,624	11,042	76,106	41,099	117,205	128,247	8,836	6,447	15,283	78,061	34,417	112,478	127,761	256,008
1900	10,315	7,443	17,758	87,041	51,096	138,137	155,895	13,906	9,095	23,001	78,230	36,268	114,498	137,499	293,404
1901	7,646	6,326	13,972	84,853	49,739	134,592	148,564	10,968	8,042	19,010	96,797	42,353	139,150	158,160	306,724
1902	7,757	5,277	13,034	91,308	53,770	145,078	158,112	12,067	8,256	20,323	99,966	48,359	148,325	168,648	326,760
1903	6,965	4,994	11,959	99,432	57,293	156,725	168,684	13,395	9,082	22,477	132,894	51,206	184,100	206,577	375,261
1904	8,235	6,112	14,347	109,469	60,797	170,266	184,613	18,249	13,086	31,335	209,191	83,065	292,256	323,591	508,204
1905	8,544	6,231	14,775	119,287	67,146	186,433	201,208	22,104	15,335	37,439	210,270	87,234	297,504	334,943	536,151
1906	8,798	6,060	14,858	125,340	74,471	199,811	214,669	16,591	11,144	27,735	179,869	74,464	254,333	282,068	496,737

[a] For 1896 and 1897 no figures are available.

The stowaway is an anomaly in immigration work and statistics. He is regarded neither as an alien nor as anything else of which the immigration officials can take cognizance. The steamship company is not permitted to land him without inspection, and the inspectors are not allowed to examine him concerning his admissibility. Unless he can effect an escape into the country from the vessel on which he has stolen passage, he must remain on board and return to the trans-oceanic port of embarkation. Table XVIII shows that during the year 607 of these anomalous individuals have arrived at certain ports of this country, and furnishes further evidence of the lengths to which aliens will go in an effort to reach this land of supposed plenty for all.

TABLE XVIII.—ALIEN STOWAWAYS, FISCAL YEAR 1906.

Port.	Number.	Port.	Number.
New York, N. Y	231	Mobile, Ala	7
Boston, Mass	61	New Orleans, La	31
Baltimore, Md	29	Norfolk, Va	24
Philadelphia, Pa	39	Pensacola, Fla	5
San Francisco, Cal	44	Portland, Me	20
San Juan, P. R	1	Savannah, Ga	14
Brunswick, Ga	1	Seattle, Wash	36
Galveston, Tex	19	Tampa, Fla	5
Honolulu, Hawaii	34		
Gulfport, Miss	6	Total	607

The alien seaman constitutes another rather anomalous class that is a source of much difficulty and embarrassment, because of the facility with which such class can escape the operation of the immigration laws by taking advantage of a status acquired under the navigation laws. The danger attaching to the situation was described in the Bureau's report for 1905 (p. 77). Another year's experience but confirms and emphasizes the need for legislation of the character then recommended. Approximately, 8,500 alien seamen have deserted from vessels arriving in ports of this country during the fiscal year 1906. That many, perhaps a majority, of them—particularly of such as were bona fide seamen—immediately reshipped on other vessels is not doubted. How many so reshipped can not be stated, or even approximated, with any degree of certainty, but that many others of these deserters did not reship, and that a large number of them were not bona fide seamen, but were aliens who had been engaged abroad as seamen for the express purpose of evading examination under the immigration laws and effecting an entry into this country despite the existence in their cases of dangerous or loathsome contagious diseases or other causes for rejection, is clearly indicated by evidence obtained both in the United States and in foreign countries.

Table XIX and XX relate to appeals taken by aliens rejected by boards of special inquiry at the ports and show action thereon by the Department, the data being arranged in the first by ports and in the second by causes of rejection.

TABLE XIX.—APPEALS FROM DECISIONS UNDER IMMIGRATION LAWS, AND ALIENS ADMITTED ON BOND, BY PORTS, FISCAL YEAR 1906.

APPEALS FROM EXCLUDING DECISIONS.

Action taken.	New York, N. Y.	Boston, Mass.	Philadelphia, Pa.	Baltimore, Md.	Montreal, Canada.	San Juan, P. R.	Seattle, Wash.	Key West, Fla.	New Orleans, La.	El Paso, Tex.	Total.
Pending at close of previous year	22	18		1							41
Appealed	3,246	372	43	54	87	1	1	4	8	5	3,821
Total	3,268	390	43	55	87	1	1	4	8	5	3,862
Disposition on appeal:											
Admitted without bond	1,323	110	3	14	30	1	1	2		1	1,485
Admitted on bond	126	17	3	1							147
Debarred	1,571	257	37	40	51			2	8	2	1,968
Withdrawn or otherwise disposed of by means other than departmental decision	147				6						153
Pending at close of current year	101	6								2	109

APPEALS FROM ADMITTING DECISIONS.

Action taken.	New York, N. Y.	Boston, Mass.	Philadelphia, Pa.	Baltimore, Md.	Montreal, Canada.	San Juan, P. R.	Seattle, Wash.	Key West, Fla.	New Orleans, La.	El Paso, Tex.	Total.
Pending at close of previous year	3	1									4
Appealed	10		5		2	1			1	1	20
Total	13	1	5		2	1			1	1	24
Disposition on appeal.											
Admitted without bond	8	1				1					10
Admitted on bond					1						1
Debarred	3		5						1	1	10
Pending at close of current year	2				1						3

ADMITTED ON BOND WITHOUT APPEAL.

Action taken.	New York, N. Y.	Boston, Mass.	Philadelphia, Pa.	Baltimore, Md.	Montreal, Canada.	San Juan, P. R.	Seattle, Wash.	Key West, Fla.	New Orleans, La.	El Paso, Tex.	Total.
Admitted			3		3						6

TABLE XX.—APPEALS FROM DECISIONS UNDER IMMIGRATION LAWS, AND ALIENS ADMITTED ON BOND, BY CAUSES, FISCAL YEAR 1906.

APPEALS FROM EXCLUDING DECISIONS.

Action taken.	Idiots.	Insane persons.[a]	Paupers or likely to become public charges.[b]	Loathsome or dangerous contagious diseases.	Convicts.	Under sec. 11, act of 1903.	Contract laborers.[c]	Total.
Pending at close of previous year	.....	.....	39	.....	.....	.....	2	41
Appealed	11	2	3,227	4	16	131	430	3,821
Total	11	2	3,266	4	16	131	432	3,862
Disposition on appeal;								
Admitted without bond	.....	1	1,313	1	2	63	105	1,485
Admitted on bond	.....	.....	147	.....	.....	.....	.....	147
Debarred during current year	11	1	1,606	3	11	52	284	1,968
Withdrawn or otherwise finally disposed of by means other than departmental decision	.....	.....	103	.....	1	8	41	153
Pending at close of current year	.....	.....	97	.....	2	8	2	109

APPEALS FROM ADMITTING DECISIONS.

Action taken.	Idiots.	Insane persons.	Paupers or likely to become public charges.	Loathsome or dangerous contagious diseases.	Convicts.	Under sec. 11, act of 1903.	Contract laborers.	Total.
Pending at close of previous year	.....	.....	2	.....	.....	1	1	4
Appealed	.....	.....	14	.....	1	.....	5	20
Total	.....	.....	16	.....	1	1	6	24
Disposition on appeal;								
Admitted without bond	.....	.....	6	.....	.....	.....	4	10
Admitted on bond	.....	.....	.....	.....	.....	.....	1	1
Debarred	.....	.....	8	.....	.....	1	1	10
Withdrawn or otherwise finally disposed of by means other than departmental decision	.....	.....	.....	.....	.....	.....	.....	.....
Pending at close of current year	.....	.....	2	.....	1	.....	.....	3

[a] Includes those who have been insane within five years; those who have had two attacks of insanity, and epileptics.
[b] Includes professional beggars.
[c] Includes those who have been debarred as contract laborers within one year.

ADMITTED ON BOND WITHOUT APPEAL........ 6

2. SOURCES OF AND INDUCEMENTS TO IMMIGRATION.

Attention has been directed in the preceding subtitle to the showing of Table III as to the sources from which the foreign blood is being drawn that is from year to year introduced into the veins of the American nation. This subject deserves the most careful consideration. It gains added importance and gravity with the advent of each year. This, in common with other phases of the immigration problem, is commanding the closest attention of the thinkers of the day. Perhaps no other public question is more generally and persistently discussed than immigration, and properly so.

In former years—that is, more particularly in decades preceding the present, we were obtaining English, Irish, Scotch, Scandinavian, and German aliens, people whose racial characteristics and ideals in the main agree with our own, and whom, therefore, we could assimilate, racially and politically, in the course of a few years. But now, taking the figures of Table III, we see that 67 per cent of our immigration during the past year consisted of aliens of those races which occupy southern and eastern Europe and Asia Minor; that about 14 per cent consisted of Hebrews (largely from Russia); that the south Italians, taken alone, constituted about 22 per cent; and that, comparatively, the introduction of aliens belonging to races akin to ours in original stock is small, for during the year the German aliens landed have amounted to less than 8 per cent of the whole, the Scandinavians to about 5 per cent, and the English, Scotch, and Irish combined to about 9.3 per cent. Whatever additional inference is drawn from these facts one thing is sure—we can not correctly hold the view that, because the Germans, Scandinavians, English, Scotch, and Irish heretofore landed on our shores have become valuable citizens within a few years, the aliens now coming that belong to distinctly different stocks can be added to our race with the same degree of success. The difference between the origin and the history of those races and our own is too great and has extended through too many ages to be overcome, even in several generations, unless under the most favorable conditions. Do not the statistics of recent years on this subject point unmistakably to the conclusion that we, as a race, are endeavoring to assimilate a large mass of almost if not quite unassimilable material?

Again, the immigration which formerly came to us from northern Europe and the British Isles was largely what might be termed a natural immigration. It was the result of an impelling ambition in the minds of a freedom-loving people to avail themselves of what they regarded as the unlimited opportunities of a new, thinly populated, and free country for that broad advancement and development denied them by the limitations of their native lands. Many of those now migrating doubtless leave their homes from like motives; but the migration of many others is the result of that general unrest that exists among the laboring classes of southern and eastern Europe, which is encouraged or even fomented by the agents of the transportation companies scouring the country for passengers. These matters have been fully covered by the former reports of the Bureau. Particular attention is called to the statements made in the last year's report under the headings "Inducements to immigration," and "Transportation lines" (pp. 48–57), completely setting forth the lengths to which those whose pecuniary interest is involved will go to produce the requisite number of passengers to pack the steerage of their vessels and pile up enough of the low-rate fares to aggregate a handsome profit from each voyage. There is no reason to believe that the evil conditions there portrayed have been in the least reduced. There is much cause to hold the opinion that they are being continued with increasing force and effect. Is it not time that some step, far in advance of anything heretofore attempted, shall be taken to effectually protect the United States at least from this forced artificial immigration? It is quite clear that the provisions of the act of 1903, prohibiting other advertising in foreign countries by passenger carriers than the dates of sailings of their vessels and the costs and facilities of passage therein, and that in the act of 1893, requiring that such carriers shall post conspicuously in their foreign ticket offices copies of the United States immigration laws printed in the language of the country where passage is sold, are not effective of their purpose. Recourse to some more drastic measure is required to effect a discontinuance of these pernicious practices which result in encouraging the discontented element of foreign countries to settle in our midst. (See also subtitle 3 of this title, below.)

In this connection the Bureau desires to repeat with emphasis its special recommendation of last year (p. 78, Annual Report 1905) for the holding of an international conference on the subjects of immigration and emigration. While it is true, at least from our point of view, that this country may be more deeply interested in these subjects than any of the countries of Europe and Asia, the Bureau believes that no difficulty should be experienced in bringing about such a convention. Viewed in their broad significance, these subjects are of a humanitarian character, and it can not reasonably be said that other countries are less interested in the personal welfare of their citizens than the United States. The enforcement of the immigration laws, under existing conditions, necessarily results in hardship and suffering on the part of those aliens who are turned back after arrival at ports of the United States. It is thought, therefore, that the countries whose subjects are affected should be willing to agree to at least certain general measures having in view the welfare of their own citizens. International conferences have been held, with beneficial and far-reaching results, on various subjects of much less importance than these. Such conferences have brought about the present international arrangements concerning postal affairs, fisheries, and various other matters of a commercial or material character; immigration and emigration affect the welfare of human beings and ought certainly to appeal as strongly to the sentiments of the various nations. To such a convention all of the countries interested to any considerable extent should be requested to send delegates of ability and experience. It is believed that the result would be a general understanding of much benefit to all concerned.

3. Physical and Mental Condition of Aliens.

Adverting to the comparative statement, given under subtitle 1 in discussing Table III (p. 8), attention is directed to the increase in the number of aliens—always considerable enough—who upon reaching our ports are found to be afflicted with contagious diseases (principally trachoma) or with idiocy or insanity. During the year also there has arrived a considerable number of persons of weak or imbecile mind—not sufficiently marked to justify a diagnosis of idiocy or insanity, but yet a serious enough defect to militate heavily against the advisability of allowing them to enter. Many of these have been rejected as persons likely to become public charges; in other cases the surrounding circumstances were such as to make a decision to that effect unreasonable, and nothing remained, under the terms of the law, but to admit the alien, notwithstanding his low mental state. Another significant feature of the year's immigration has been the vast number who upon arrival have been described by the examining surgeons as "persons of poor physique," a term which is not perhaps always clearly understood by those not connected with the Immigration Service. The significance of a certificate for poor physique rendered by a Public Health and Marine-Hospital surgeon is shown by the following definition of the term furnished by one of those officers:

> A certificate of this nature implies that the alien concerned is afflicted with a body not only but illy adapted to the work necessary to earn his bread, but also but poorly able to withstand the onslaught of disease. It means that he is undersized, poorly developed, with feeble heart action, arteries below the standard size; that he is physically degenerate, and as such not only unlikely to become a desirable citizen, but also very likely to transmit his undesirable qualities to his offspring should he, unfortunately for the country in which he is domiciled, have any.
>
> Of all causes for rejection, outside of those for dangerous, contagious, or loathsome diseases, or for mental disease, that of "poor physique" should receive the most weight, for in admitting such aliens not only do we increase the number of public charges by their inability to gain their bread through their physical inaptitude and their low resistance to disease, but we admit likewise progenitors to this country whose offspring will reproduce, often in an exaggerated degree, the physical degeneracy of their parents.

That the physical and mental quality of the aliens we are now receiving is much below that of those who have come in former years is evident. It is of the utmost importance to the future welfare of this country that the standard in these respects should be raised to and kept at a high point. Persons who are below that standard, either physically or mentally, should never be allowed to embark for the United States. Many of the cases are those of large families, one or two of the children connected with which are weak-minded or of poor physique. Those families should be required either not to migrate from their homes with the purpose of entering the United States or else to leave the weak members behind.

The dangers attendant upon the bringing to our ports, in the steerage with other aliens, of those afflicted with contagious diseases have been described in previous reports of the Bureau. The disease of most frequent occurrence, trachoma, does not develop in an infected person for a considerable time after the infection occurs. Therefore the presence in the close quarters of the steerage of a vessel of a few persons afflicted with the disease may quite probably result in the landing of several hundred infected aliens, a sufficient length of time not having elapsed to permit of the detection of the disease. That the only measure at their disposal, viz, the fining (under section 9 of the immigration act) of steamship companies bringing such aliens, is being employed extensively by administrative officers is indicated by the following table, showing that $24,300 have been collected during the year for violations of said law.

FINES CERTIFIED UNDER SECTION 9, FISCAL YEAR 1906.

Port.	July.	August.	September.	October.	November.	December.
Baltimore	....	$200	....	....	....	$100
Boston	....	....	$300	$300	$100	100
Ellis Island	$4,500	2,000	300	1,000	600	600
Galveston	....	100	....	....	....	....
Jacksonville	100	....	....	....	....	....
Key West	....	100	100	200	....	100
New Orleans	300	....	....	....	....	....
Philadelphia	100	....	400	....	....	300
San Francisco	100	100	....	200	100	....
Seattle	300	100	....	....	....	....
Total	5,400	2,600	1,100	1,700	800	1,200

FINES CERTIFIED UNDER SECTION 9, FISCAL YEAR 1906—Continued.

Port.	January.	February.	March.	April.	May.	June.	Total.
Baltimore	$300	$100		$100	$200	$200	$1,200
Boston	300		$500	200			1,800
Ellis Island	200	600	1,100	700	2,000	3,200	16,800
Galveston	200			100			400
Jacksonville							100
Key West						100	600
New Orleans	100			100			500
Philadelphia	200		100	400			1,500
San Francisco	100		100				700
Seattle					300		700
Total	1,400	700	1,800	1,600	2,500	3.500	24,300

It is apparent, however, that as a preventive measure this fine is not a success. It does not insure the adoption of the requisite precautions to prevent the sale of passage to afflicted aliens, it often being less expensive for the transportation company to take the risk of having to pay a few fines than to employ the proper number of skilled medical examiners at the port of embarkation. Therefore the Bureau repeats the recommendation contained in last year's report, that unless some arrangement can be effected whereby Public Health and Marine-Hospital surgeons of this Government can be stationed abroad to inspect aliens prior to embarkation the fine for bringing to a port of this country an alien afflicted with a dangerous or a loathsome contagious disease be increased from $100 to $500. This would probably compel the transportation companies, as a measure of economy, to observe proper care with regard to the medical inspection of prospective passengers. The ideal plan for controlling this situation, however, is the one that has been urged by the Bureau for years, i. e., the stationing of United States medical officers abroad, with the requirement that all prospective passengers shall be examined and passed by them as physically and mentally fit for landing in this country. This would prevent the emigration, not only of those afflicted with contagious diseases, but also of those afflicted with idiocy and insanity. As a measure of humanity, from the point of view of the alien, such medical officers should, perhaps, be stationed in the interior of the foreign countries, attached to our consulates, the understanding being that none should leave their home with the intent of proceeding to the United States until supplied with a bill of health from one of these physicians. Possibly the inauguration of such an arrangement might be practically difficult, although it would seem reasonable to expect that the governments of the foreign countries from which aliens migrate to the United States would be glad of an opportunity to cooperate with the latter in measures intended to prevent the hardships and disappointments suffered by such of the citizens of those countries as are turned back at our ports after having abandoned their homes and made long and expensive journeys by rail and water. Locating the examiners at the principal foreign seaports of embarkation would quite as effectively cure the evil, so far as we are directly concerned, and would at the same time afford a large measure of protection to the alien by preventing a long, tedious, and eventually fruitless ocean voyage.

The adoption of the above-mentioned plan, moreover, would produce a valuable indirect effect, viz, the discouragement of the belief so prevalent among the classes from which the bulk of our immigration is drawn that it is an easy matter to obtain passage to and enter this country, and the defeat to a great extent of the schemes of the "runners" and "promoters" so extensively employed, if not immediately by the steamship companies, by their ticket agents on a commission basis. With this same object in view the laws of this country relating to immigration should be published in the languages of the various countries of Europe and extensively distributed, thus advertising the difficulties which are thrown in the way of the undesirable classes. It would not of course be necessary nor perhaps wise to publish the various acts in their entirety; but, to prevent confusion, and to insure at least a reasonable opportunity for all concerned to thoroughly inform themselves on the subject, the salient features of existing laws, in as concrete a form as possible, should be so translated and published and distributed.

4. Distribution of Aliens.

So far as aliens of the desirable classes are concerned, a solution of the immigration problem does not consist so much in bringing about a reduction in numbers—for there is yet room in this country for the right kind of settlers—as in securing, by some means, a proper distribution of those who come to us. By referring to Table VII (p. 23) it will be seen that during the fiscal year just closed, as in previous years, the bulk of the aliens have avowedly been destined to a few of our large centers of population; that 374,708, or over one-third of the entire number, claimed the State of New York as their ultimate destination; that 198,681, or over one-sixth of the whole, asserted they were going to Pennsylvania; that 86,539, or about one-twelfth, were avowedly destined to Illinois; that 73,863 intended to reside in Massachusetts; and that 58,415 were en route to New Jersey. While these figures are taken from advance information given by the aliens at the time of their admission, they are without doubt sufficiently accurate to furnish a fair basis of computation on the subject. Carrying the calculation no further than the foregoing, we discover that over seven-tenths of the aliens admitted during the fiscal year 1906 indicated an intention to settle in already thickly populated districts, and doubtless the majority of them actually did take up residences in the several large cities located in the States mentioned. All the while that this congestion of certain centers is occurring, the Bureau is being importuned by the agricultural, mining, manufacturing, and railroad interests of the thinly populated sections of the country, and even by some of the States, for advice as to how some part of this immigration can be turned to the localities where farmers, miners, and laborers are needed. The Bureau has replied that it stands constantly ready to aid by any lawful means in the accomplishment of this laudable object and has offered such suggestions as seemed appropriate. It has especially encouraged the idea advanced by the representatives of the immigration bureaus of some of the Southern States that direct trans-Atlantic communication by steamer be established between some of the larger southern ports and European ports, so that aliens might be diverted southward before ever leaving their homes, and kept out of the path in following which so many become stranded among the "colonies" established in our large northern cities. It is true in the vast majority of cases that the alien has determined in advance, at least tentatively, upon his future place of settlement.

Another plan which has been advocated by many and to which some space was devoted in the last report of the Bureau, is the proper representation at Ellis Island of the advantages offered settlers by the different sections of the country. That much could thus be immediately accomplished, at least with the alien who has not predetermined his future residence, there can be no doubt, but the chief benefits of such a plan would, it is believed, be gradually developed—for, as a few of the arriving aliens were deflected to a point where needed a nucleus would be formed to which larger numbers would be attracted in succeeding years.

As the subject was fully discussed in last year's report (p. 58) it requires no further comment or explanation here. Another year's experience has but emphasized the need, if the present large immigration is to continue, for making use of every available device to discourage the "colonization" of these foreigners in the large cities and to so distribute them as to render their perfect assimilation possible and secure such benefit to the country as is obtainable by adding to its producing population.

5. Alien Contract Laborers.

The steady and increasing demand for labor, particularly in some of the least thickly populated districts of the country, and the difficulties attendant upon inducing the immigrants of the laboring classes to proceed to those localities where their services are most urgently required, combined with the ever strong desire of the employer to obtain labor at the lowest world-market price, have doubtless resulted in the importation during the year in violation of law of a considerable number of aliens under contract or promise of employment. The difficulties of enforcing this feature of the immigration laws, alluded to in former reports of the Bureau and particularly described in that for 1905 (pp. 44–46), have been quite as great during the past as in any preceding year. Yet the inspectors at the ports and on the land boundaries detected and turned back 2,314 such contract laborers, about twice as many as in the fiscal year 1905. Approximately 18 per cent of the entire number of rejections, therefore, were upon this ground. When it is remembered how in this class of cases the inspector must, as a rule, obtain from the alien himself a confession of the fact that he has been induced to migrate by a promise of employment, and how readily by means of coaching this source of evidence can be destroyed by those interested to violate the law—especially as the aliens thus imported are usually members of the more intelligent classes—the only wonder is that the officers have been skillful enough to apprehend so large a number; and the obvious conclusion must be that more escaped than were detected and deported.

Nothing more than the average success has attended the Bureau's efforts of the past year to punish those guilty of importing laborers. That average, as pointed out in the last annual report, is very low, but through no fault of the Bureau, which has always exerted every possible endeavor to make the alien contract labor law effective of its purpose, not only by the detection of those who attempt to enter the country in violation thereof, but by the much more salutary method of appropriately punishing those guilty of producing the migration of aliens by putting forth "offers, solicitations, or promises." Of the several important prosecutions mentioned in last year's report, that against the Ellsworth Coal Company was discontinued in August, 1905, the witnesses having all dispersed since the date of the inception of the case, October, 1903, and that against the San Francisco Brick Company, which originated in October, 1902, was, according to recent accounts, still pending in court. Many cases of minor importance have been investigated or prosecuted, but two stand out with particular prominence in the year's work. A suit was brought in November, 1905, against the Tile Grate and Mantel Association of New York for importing ten tile setters, the result of which was a confession of judgment by the defendants in the sum of $4,000 and costs, the ten aliens, of course, being deported after having been held for use as witnesses. And the Aultman Company, of Canton, Ohio, was prosecuted for importing certain ironmolders from Canada, the case arising in the fall of 1904. Several searching investigations were made by the Bureau, and when the case was finally brought to trial in February, 1906, a decision was rendered holding that, the particular alien involved having been domiciled in this country for some time preceding the date of his employment by the company in Canada, he could not be considered an alien in the sense of the contract labor laws, and that therefore the company was guilty of no offense. From this sweeping decision an appeal has been taken and the Bureau hopes a reversal may be obtained in the higher court.

What are believed to have been two extensive schemes to secure foreign labor have come to light in the past year, and are at the date of this report being investigated by the Bureau. The evidence is already at hand to show that some individual or corporation is engaged in importing numbers of Japanese laborers to work on the railroads of the Northwest. The plan is cunningly devised and persistently, accurately, and so far successfully carried out. The Japanese Government will issue passports to only a limited number of its citizens destined to mainland ports of the United States, but it is less difficult for such citizens to secure passports if going to the Hawaiian Islands. Numbers of Japanese laborers come to Hawaii, destined to "hotels" kept by labor agents, and consistently claim under examination by immigrant inspectors that they are merely seekers for such labor as can be secured in the islands; that they have made no advance arrangements for employment either in the islands or on the mainland, and that they are not in any sense contract laborers. Nothing remains but to admit them, as conditions on the islands and the robust physique of the applicants would make it unreasonable to hold that they are likely to become public charges, and it is impossible to develop any evidence of what the inspectors feel morally certain exists, viz, a contract to proceed eventually to the mainland and accept prearranged employment. After such aliens are admitted they remain a few days or weeks in Hawaii and then ship for northwestern ports. Having already been admitted to the United States at the Hawaiian port their voyage thence is "coastwise," and they can not be examined upon arrival at the mainland port under the alien contract or any other provision of the immigration laws. Japanese immigration direct to San Francisco from Japan has fallen during the year to a very small figure, doubtless from causes similar to those mentioned above, for the commissioner at San Francisco reports that Japanese have been arriving there coastwise from Honolulu and from Canadian ports at the rate of 1,000 to 3,000 per month. That several thousand laborers have been imported under this evasion of the law is not doubted. In administering the alien contract labor, as well as other features of the immigration laws, the Bureau is always careful to avoid action that could by any possibility be regarded as a discrimination against aliens of a particular race. The alien contract labor law applies to the Japanese in the same manner and to the same extent as to European aliens, and the identical policy is followed in enforcing its provisions, whether the aliens affected are of the English, German, Italian, Japanese, or any other nationality. The Bureau's efforts in this line are directed to the prevention of the importation of foreign laborers under contract or agreement to perform service in this country whatever their race; and it is of course anxious to bring about a discontinuance of the above-mentioned extensive evasion of the law by discovering and properly dealing with the parties in this country responsible for the importation of the laborers, and is endeavoring to do so by every means at its command. The propriety is suggested of bringing the matter to the attention of the Japanese Government.

The other instance arose in the Southwest. In the past it has been the practice of the several railroads of that section to employ numbers of Mexican peons as track hands. These peons would cross the border by thousands and would then be engaged by labor agents to proceed to various points where their services were required. This past spring the supply of such laborers has not equaled the demand, partly because of a considerable increase in the latter and partly by reason of the more successful enforcement of the general provisions of the immigration laws at the border ports. The competition for laborers produced by this scarcity became sufficient to cause an advance from $1 to $1.25 in the average daily wage. Certain labor agencies have been importuning the Bureau in this matter, claiming that the welfare of the entire Southwest depends upon their being able to supply the demand for labor on the railroads, and that it is impossible to obtain the labor elsewhere than in Mexico; also that being unable to procure such unskilled labor in this country they are entitled to import it under the proviso to section 2 of the act of March 3, 1903, "that skilled labor may be imported if labor of like kind unemployed can not be found in this country." It is needless to say that the Bureau will accord the subject careful investigation and consideration both as to the facts and the law.[a]

[a] Since the close of the year to which this report relates, but prior to its going to press, the investigation of the case of the southwestern railroads was completed, and the Attorney-General was called upon for an opinion whether (1) ordinary hands commonly employed in the construction and maintenance of the tracks of railroads are "skilled laborers" within the meaning of the term as used in section 2 of the immigration act of March 3, 1903; and (2) whether, if not such "skilled laborers," workmen of the character mentioned can be lawfully imported into the United States under contract, even if like labor unemployed can not be found in this country. After reviewing comprehensively the various provisions of law relating to alien contract laborers and

6. The Canadian and Mexican Borders.

As regards the enforcement of both the immigration and Chinese exclusion laws, a striking contrast exists between the conditions on our northern and our southern boundaries. The enforcement of the Chinese exclusion laws on those borders is fully discussed in subtitle 12 of Title II (p. 93). With the Dominion of Canada, and with the various land and water transportation companies of that country, the Bureau has arrangements that make it possible to handle in a most satisfactory manner the large numbers of aliens who come to Canadian ports destined to the United States, or who seek to enter this country after a short period of residence in Canada; while the opposite is true concerning Mexico and the Mexican transportation companies (see Table III C, p. 15). The entire Canadian border, as well as all of the Canadian ports on the Atlantic and Pacific, is now under the jurisdiction of the United States commissioner of immigration for Canada, whose headquarters are located at Montreal. The Bureau has been uniformly fortunate in the character of the men who have filled that position since its creation, and the position of chief assistant to such commissioner. The present commissioner was the second in charge under the former occupant of the office, and has proved a worthy successor, while his assistant has demonstrated during the past year that his selection for the post was a wise one. If space permitted the report received from Montreal covering the past year would be extensively quoted, but the Bureau must be content with giving elsewhere (subtitle 8 of this title, p. 72) a digest of its

---

the judicial decisions rendered thereunder, and discussing the distinction between skilled and unskilled laborers, the Attorney-General expressed the following opinion:

"The act [of March 3, 1903] was designed and intended for the protection and security of the American laborer, whose welfare every patriotic citizen is bound to promote. Laws designed for his benefit should, if possible, be so construed as to effectuate rather than retard the objects for which they were enacted.

"The legislation with which we are now concerned has been on the statute books in substantially its present form for more than twenty years. As previously pointed out, the original act divided labor into two classes, skilled and unskilled. It first denounced the bringing in of either class under contract. For reasons of public policy Congress then excepted from the operation of the law skilled labor on new industries. The courts having intimated that the law was designed to apply to unskilled labor only, Congress took occasion to make clear its intent. The act of 1903 contains the unequivocal provision that the act shall apply to skilled as well as unskilled labor. In this act, which is now in force, the distinction between the two classes of labor is still maintained. It is therein provided that neither class shall be brought in under contract. No exception whatever is contained in the act in respect to unskilled labor, but it is provided that skilled labor may be imported under certain conditions. That there is a difference in fact and in law between skilled and unskilled labor is too plain to admit of argument.

"It must also be presumed that Congress was mindful of this difference in the enactment of this law. It is certainly not for the executive department of the Government to nullify the will of Congress by declining or failing to give the words of the act their natural and logical import. Especially is this true in a case involving the welfare of such a very large number of our own citizens. Moreover, it does not appear that since the enactment of this law in 1885 it has ever before been contended that unskilled alien contract labor could legally be imported.

"The determination of the question as to what is skilled and what unskilled labor within the meaning of the law rests largely with you. I entertain no doubt, however, that 'ordinary hands, commonly employed in the construction and maintenance of the tracks of railroads,' are not skilled laborers within the meaning of the immigration act of March 3, 1903. Having reached the conclusion that they are not skilled laborers it follows from what I have previously said that such laborers may not 'be imported into this country under contract in any event.' "

contents. It shows that the law is being enforced along our northern boundary with the same diligence and success as heretofore. It would, of course, be extravagant to claim that no aliens enter unlawfully from Canada; but it is believed that the evil is reduced to the minimum, considering the long border line that must be guarded.

With the Mexican border the difficulties are constantly on the increase. From year to year, in fact, from month to month, the evidences of evasion of our laws there multiply; and the very worst elements of the foreigners enter by that route. Aliens who are so diseased, or of such frail physique, or so apparently paupers, as to convince even the interested steamship companies of the risk attendant upon trying to enter them at Atlantic seaports are sent by the steamship agents to Mexico, and from there enter surreptitiously across the border under the guidance of promoters located in Mexico, or, after treatment by local physicians and temporary "cures" of their maladies, secure admission at the border ports. This is a favorite route for the Syrian immigrants, among whom trachoma is such a common disease. It is known that many aliens who have been rejected on former occasions at the seaports of the United States proceed to Mexico to again try to enter despite our objection. Because of the length of the border line and the natural impediments to a sufficiently close patrol of it to insure even to a reasonable certainty that it is being successfully guarded, and the ease with which the operations of the promoters can be continued in Mexico, the problem is one which, in the Bureau's opinion, could not be solved even by doubling the present considerable force of officers there stationed. It is believed that much good would be accomplished, by way of discouraging the migration of these undesirable classes to Mexico, if the suggestion advanced last year by the President, viz, that the Mexican border be closed to all aliens except citizens of the Republic of Mexico, should be adopted. On this subject the following is quoted from the report of the inspector in charge at El Paso:

> In view of the fact that all taxable aliens who are refused admission at this port remain upon the Mexican side of the border until they can enter surreptitiously, and inasmuch as large numbers of Syrian and other undesirable aliens who would not be admitted at our seaports are constantly moving toward the border to enter illegally, if necessary, it is believed that the recommendation of the President to the last Congress, that aliens other than residents of Mexico should not be allowed to enter the United States across the Mexican border, should be adopted at the earliest possible moment.

The gravity of this situation has been fully disclosed in prior reports of the Bureau. That some drastic measure is required is obvious.

7. Immigrant Stations.

The commissioner of immigration and the surgeon in charge of the medical inspection of aliens at Ellis Island in their annual reports speak of several improvements, by rearrangement, in the facilities for handling the arriving aliens promptly and efficiently, particularly the examination of them by the doctors. A change is being effected in the hospital building at said station so as to provide separate quarters for detaining and examining aliens supposed to be afflicted with insanity. The building of an additional island on which a hospital for contagious diseases is to be located has been completed, and gratifying progress has been made concerning the construction of the hospital itself. If immigration is to continue at the rate shown for the past several years, the general accommodations at Ellis Island will need to be much improved and extended. With present facilities; no more than 5,000 aliens can be, and not nearly so many should be, examined in a day; but on some days in March, April, and May last as many as 20,000 were awaiting examination at that port. The commissioner at Ellis Island having submitted certain recommendations for changes in the buildings at that station, the Commissioner-General, with the approval of the Secretary, requested the Supervising Architect of the Treasury Department to accompany him on a thorough inspection of the said buildings. The result was a confirmation of the view theretofore expressed by the commissioner that the accommodations available in the said buildings are totally inadequate to a proper conduct of the inspection work of that port. The buildings should be extensively changed and remodeled in order to adapt them to the making of the inspections in the minimum time, with a minimum amount of labor and expense, and with comfort and convenience to all concerned. Various improvements are needed in the rooms provided for the feeding of the detained aliens, and also in the sleeping quarters, dormitories, etc. The Supervising Architect, after carefully considering the matter, believes that an appropriation of $400,000 would be required to put the buildings in the condition that is emphatically demanded by existing circumstances. It is therefore urged that an appropriation of this sum be requested at as early a date as possible. The need is imperative and should be promptly met. When the buildings were originally constructed, of course it was not imagined that the business would increase so rapidly and to such a great extent, else, doubtless, they would have been built and arranged upon quite a different scale and plan. In order that another mistake of the same character, the evil results of which would be realized even in a less period of time, may not be made in constructing the new contagious-disease hospital, it is important that a further appropriation shall be secured therefor. Even in the short time that has elapsed since the original appropriation of $250,000 was made for the building of this hospital, the needs of the service have grown to a considerable extent. The increase in immigration brings a corresponding increase in the danger of the spread of disease among detained aliens. In carrying the already commenced construction of the hospital to completion, therefore, it should be built large enough and sufficiently commodious and complete in its arrangement and equipment to obviate any possibility of additions or extensions being required in the near future. To finish it in this manner and with this assurance, a further appropriation of $250,000 will be necessary, and it is hoped it may be promptly obtained at the forthcoming session of Congress.

Another respect in which an improvement is urgently required is with regard to the refrigerating and cold storage plant at the Ellis Island station. The one now in use, when built, was adequate for the existing needs. It was originally installed as a 2-ton plant, but as a matter of fact during a part of the time has been required to do the work of a 3½-ton plant. The cold storage facilities thus afforded are barely sufficient to preserve a day's supply of food in the busy season, and this close margin would be the cause of much suffering if for any reason it should be impossible to communicate with the mainland for a longer period than a day. Moreover, the needs in this respect will be still further increased by the completion of the new hospital for contagious diseases. To place the ice plant and cold storage facilities in proper condition an appropriation of $30,000 would be required, and in the opinion of the Bureau should be promptly made.

Yet another matter of importance requires action by Congress. The ferryboat *Ellis Island*, which for more than two years past has been used for hourly trips from the barge office on the mainland to the station on the island, is beginning to show the effects of this constant service without opportunity to rest or even to be laid off duty for sufficient periods to permit of proper repairs being made as required from time to time. While the service has been fortunate since the *Ellis Island* was placed in commission in not having any serious accidents, there can be no assurance that this good fortune will continue, and there should be available for alternate use another boat of equal capacity. This would be, in the ultimate, a measure of economy, as the boat would last much longer if occasionally taken out of commission and repaired, painted, etc. It is therefore recommended that an appropriation of $115,000 be obtained for the construction of another boat of the same general style and equipment as the *Ellis Island*. This is also an urgent matter and the Bureau believes should have early attention in the interest both of good administration and of economy.

At Boston a slight addition has been made to the detention quarters to extend to proper proportions the facilities for feeding immigrants, and the commissioner states the accommodations are adequate for present needs.

The commissioner at Philadelphia calls attention in his annual report to the need of a suitable immigrant station at that port. Under the existing arrangement, the offices of the commissioner and his assistants are located in one building, the examination rooms in another, and the detention quarters in a third, the inconvenience of which is apparent. Unless an interested transportation company can be induced to construct a suitably situated building, he suggests that it would be well to secure Congressional approval of the purchase of a site and the erection of appropriate quarters, in all of which the Bureau heartily concurs.

Work on the preliminary stages of constructing an immigrant station on Angel Island, San Francisco, was interrupted by the earthquake. All things considered, however, satisfactory progress is being made with the work. The need for such a station has not been reduced by the catastrophe which for a while threatened San Francisco's commercial supremacy, for the bringing of Chinese and other aliens to that port has already begun to reassume its former proportions.

Plans for the construction of suitable buildings for the accommodation of arriving aliens at New Orleans, La., Galveston, Tex., and Portland, Me., are now taking definite shape, and it is hoped that by the close of another year these much-needed stations will be in use. In each of these instances the buildings will be constructed by the transportation companies. Plans are also being perfected for the removal of the immigrant station for the Puget Sound district from Port Townsend to Seattle, and when the contemplated arrangement is effected it is believed that it will be possible to handle in an ideal manner the large immigration now coming through that district.

A new immigrant station was occupied at El Paso, Tex., during the year, and much-needed facilities for enforcing the law at that important port are now available. The great improvement afforded by the use of this building is acknowledged by all in that section, and the inspectors are able to perform their duties with much greater comfort to themselves and to the aliens as well. Some additional improvements have been made to the excellent station now in use at Honolulu in the way of beautifying the grounds by which it is surrounded, all being accomplished without cost to the immigrant fund. The service now has at that port convenient, comfortable quarters; in fact, an ideal station.

8. Reports of Commissioners and Inspectors in Charge.

The accounts of the past year's work which have reached the Bureau from the various commissioners of immigration and inspectors in charge are replete with information of interest and value. If the limits within which it is desired to keep this report permitted, extensive quotations would be given from them. Under existing circumstances, however, all that can be incorporated is a recital of some of the most salient points covered.

The commissioner at Ellis Island, in calling attention to the unprecedented immigration through his port, emphasizes the fact that the examination of tourists and transits, and of some of the alleged American citizens, requires as much time and care as the examination of the immigrant alien. He states that he believes the large increase in the number of insane persons, idiots, and convicts detected at his port is due, not to an increase in the number of such persons leaving foreign countries, but to the better inspection that is being maintained; that 10 per cent of the number of aliens arriving at Ellis Island were detained for hearing before boards of special inquiry, and that for a protracted period during the year an average of 1,500 persons were detained in the station daily, requiring the constant care to which such wards are entitled. Also that the unprecedented work of the year has been performed with due regularity and without the complaints and adverse criticisms which all too frequently characterize undertakings of this nature, all of which is a striking testimonial to the character and ability of the officers employed at said station. Concerning the work of the medical officers, the commissioner makes a statement which it is thought, in justice to those efficient, painstaking Government officials, should be quoted:

> The report of the surgeon in charge accompanying this report is too replete with evidence of thoroughness of investigation to need much or any comment on my part, but it is, nevertheless, a very great pleasure to me to thus acknowledge my indebtedness to that very important service. It would be extremely difficult for me to overstate the important service they have rendered the Government, the helpful assistance they have given to afflicted aliens, and the careful and fearless manner in which they have detected and diagnosed multiform cases of disease, many of them of a contagious nature.

The commissioner at Boston calls attention to the volume of work that has been satisfactorily performed at his port and the subport of New Bedford; describes the peculiar conditions under which the inspection of aliens has to be made because of docking arrangements in Boston Harbor, and the fact that this entails additional duties upon the officers; cites the number of instances in which perjury committed by aliens in Boston interested in securing the landing of friends and relatives has been detected and punished; also to the manner in which a strict investigation of naturalization frauds has discouraged the use of fictitious naturalization certificates; and to the practical breaking up of the former extensive practice of smuggling aliens into the various small seaports of the New England States. He incloses a comprehensive and able report from the surgeon in charge of the medical inspection of aliens at Boston, in which that officer explains in detail the manner in which the inspections are made, indicating a thoroughness that is both commendable and gratifying.

The commissioner of immigration at Philadelphia submits a report covering the various details of the work performed at his station during the year, showing that the law has been carefully and rigidly enforced at the said port without friction or complaint; also that several important prosecutions of persons engaged in the unlawful importation of aliens have been conducted, and that in some instances the courts have ruled to the disadvantage of the Government. He also speaks in the highest terms of the capacity and thoroughness of the Public Health and Marine-Hospital surgeon in charge of the medical inspections at his port. Altogether, his report is most gratifying, indicating, as it does, that the officers at Philadelphia are performing their duties under the law intelligently and successfully.

From the commissioner at Baltimore a gratifying summary of the year's work is received, showing that, while the immigration through his port fell considerably below the figures of the preceding year, the inspection of aliens has been conducted in a very thorough manner. He also commends in unmeasured terms the assistance rendered by the Public Health and Marine-Hospital surgeon at his port.

The summaries forwarded by the commissioner of immigration for Canada show that the year has witnessed a continuation of the good work which has so long been performed by the branch of the service which is located in that foreign contiguous country. The duties to be performed by the inspectors there stationed are varied and peculiarly difficult, because of the fact that Canada and the United States being so closely related commercially the utmost care must be exercised to enforce the law without in any way interfering with the business of the two countries and of the people residing each side of the boundary line. As already stated, this report shows—which is a sufficient commendation in itself—that the work has been kept up to the usual high standard.

Immigration to Porto Rico has both increased as to numbers and improved as to the character of the aliens, according to an interesting report received from the commissioner at San Juan. He also states that generally satisfactory conditions prevail, and that there is no reason to suppose they will not continue.

The considerable reduction in the total number of aliens entering the country through San Francisco is said by the commissioner at that port to be due to a variety of causes, one of which is, of course, the catastrophe which visited San Francisco in April last, and another the fact that a considerable part of the Japanese immigration which formerly came through that port has been deflected to Hawaii and thence to the northwest section of the mainland (see subtitle 5 of this title).

His report also shows that the immigration work devolving upon his office has been ably and successfully handled without any cause for complaint.

From the inspectors in charge at the various smaller ports, and especially those at New Orleans, El Paso, Seattle, and Honolulu, very gratifying accounts of the occurrences of the past year reach the Bureau. This is also true of the more important interior stations, such as Chicago and St. Louis.

9. Financial Statement.

Receipts and Expenditures on Account of the Immigrant Fund for the Fiscal Year July 1, 1905, to June 30, 1906, and Approximate Balance on Hand June 30, 1906.

Approximate balance June 30, 1905		$1,841,044.53
Receipts fiscal year 1906		2,290,901.56
Total		4,131,946.09
Expenditures fiscal year 1906		1,571,280.01
		2,560,666.08
Act approved March 3, 1903: For extension and addition to hospital; ferryboat; sundries, additions, repairs and alterations to Government property; and construction of new island—amount of appropriation, $380,500; balance June 30, 1906, $109,887.33; amount expended fiscal year 1906	$99,296.14	
Act approved April 28, 1904: For widening ferry house; dredging; and construction of tugboat—amount of appropriation, $94,000; balance June 30, 1906, $25,297.70; amount expended fiscal year 1906	15.65	
Act approved March 3, 1905: For constructing a detention station on Angel Island, San Francisco Harbor—amount of appropriation, $200,000; balance June 30, 1906, $199,888.49; amount expended fiscal year 1906	111.51	
Act approved March 3, 1905: For constructing a contagious-disease hospital on the proposed new island, Ellis Island, N. Y.—amount of appropriation, $250,000; balance June 30, 1906, $249,994.75; amount expended fiscal year 1906	5.25	
Amount of special appropriations to be reimbursed from the "immigrant fund"		99,428.55
Approximate balance June 30, 1906		2,461,237.53

Itemized Statement of Receipts and Expenditures at the Various Ports.

Port.	Receipts.	Apparent receipts.[a]	Expenditures.
Astoria, Oreg	$34.00		$29.50
Baltimore, Md	109,394.00	$0.80	36,997.14
Bangor, Me	24.00		144.00
Beaufort, S. C	4.00		
Boston, Mass	135,922.75	11.44	68,898.97
Brownsville, Tex	132.00		6,948.03
Brunswick, Ga	180.00		1,625.31
Cedar Keys, Fla	6.00		
Charleston, S. C	100.00		1,874.35
Corpus Christi, Tex	2,432.00		
Eagle Pass, Tex	576.00		15,795.70
Ellis Island, N. Y	1,818,656.71	108,921.11	805,090.93
El Paso, Tex	3,744.00	.20	18,423.22
Fernandina, Fla	62.00		2,250.15
Galveston, Tex	13,038.00		6,218.45
Gulfport, Miss	574.00		1,871.81
Honolulu, Hawaii	21,051.10		28,755.20
Jacksonville, Fla	74.00		3,420.13
Juneau, Alaska	152.00		
Key West, Fla	4,968.00	3.50	4,894.40
Los Angeles, Cal	146.00		2,074.45
Marquette, Mich	48.00		
Miscellaneous		653.55	531,446.98
Mobile, Ala	1,156.00		4,277.51
Montreal, Canada	92,604.00		33,761.94
New Bedford, Mass	4,616.00	14.65	6,467.46

[a] Apparent receipts represent amounts recovered on account of overpayments, disallowances made by the Auditor, and repayments to the appropriation from various sources.

ITEMIZED STATEMENT OF RECEIPTS AND EXPENDITURES AT THE VARIOUS PORTS—Continued.

Port.	Receipts.	Apparent receipts.	Expenditures.
New Orleans, La.	$5,956.00		$10,110.17
Newport News, Va.	586.00		42.75
Nogales, Ariz.	784.00		1,356.15
Norfolk, Va.	336.00	$1.35	5,506.66
Pensacola, Fla.	640.00		2,182.70
Philadelphia, Pa.	47,700.00	38.79	31,998.15
Porto Rico	3,702.00	.76	7,689.30
Portland, Me.	1,750.00		2,986.15
Portland, Oreg.	478.00		3,200.34
Port Townsend, Wash.	5,448.00	16.75	7,126.60
Providence, R. I.	96.00		12.90
San Diego, Cal.	372.00		2,003.55
San Francisco, Cal.	12,907.00		20,424.79
Savannah, Ga.	312.00		1,511.37
Tampa, Fla.	120.00	.15	3,525.85
Wilmington, Del.	4.00		
Wilmington, N. C.	16.00		
	2,290,901.56	109,663.05	1,680,943.06
Less apparent receipts			109,663.05
Total	2,290,901.56		1,571,280.01

From the foregoing statement it will be seen that the net balance on hand, after payment of all expenses incident to the administration of the laws and regulations in regard to immigration, and of the sum of $99,428.55 for improvements and alterations, new island, etc., at Ellis Island Immigrant Station, and for construction of immigrant station, San Francisco Harbor, is $2,461,237.53. This is an increase over the balance on hand at the corresponding period last year of $620,193. The total expenditures for the execution of the immigration laws at the various points named in the foregoing table, exclusive of payments from special appropriations referred to, were $1,571,280.01.

The discrepancy between the preceding figures and those furnished by the fiscal representative of the Department of Commerce and Labor is explained by the fact that the former represent the amount of vouchers approved for payment—some of which remain unpaid—while the latter represent actual disbursements from July 1, 1905, to June 30, 1906.

II. CHINESE EXCLUSION

1. IN GENERAL.

With regard to the enforcement of the Chinese exclusion laws at the ports, along the land boundaries, and throughout the country the Bureau is able to report that it has been proceeding with this work as thoroughly and extensively as circumstances would permit. That anything particularly striking has been accomplished can not be said; but it is believed that, in the main, the officers of this service have been able, quietly and unostentatiously, to advance a few steps at least in the performance of their duties in this respect. The law is difficult of enforcement under the most favorable circumstances, but when a feeling of unrest and discontent is rife among those affected by its enforcement; when their sympathizers abroad are making use of every device, including the dangerous two-edged weapon, the boycott; when a certain element of the educated, enlightened populace of this country (the very class which it would seem reasonable to expect to approve an efficient enforcement of law) is crying out against any efforts that contemplate more than a formal, perfunctory compliance with the bare letter of the statutes; when a considerable part of the press, without troubling to ascertain facts, but upon wholly erroneous assumptions, is attacking the inspectors charged by law and their oath of office with its administration—when all these combine, as they did during part of the year, the only wonder is that the force of Chinese inspectors was not demoralized, and the fact that a fair measure of success has been attained is an eloquent testimonial to the character and endurance of the officers and to the discipline and morale that the Bureau has maintained among them.

Every possible effort has been exerted to extend to Chinese of the classes entitled by treaty provisions to enter the United States exactly the same treatment as is accorded Europeans; so that the business men, the teachers, the students, and the travelers of China have been as welcome to enter our gates as similar persons from other foreign countries.

During the past winter Congress called for a statement of what the records of the Bureau show regarding the enforcement of the Chinese exclusion laws. A compilation was furnished which contains everything of interest shown by its files, and the Bureau points with pride to that document (House Document No. 847, Fifty-ninth Congress, first session), which is a frank statement of facts capable of demonstration, and a perusal of which, it is confidently believed, must convince any fair-minded person that the Bureau has, through its officers, endeavored in good faith to administer the laws justly and in accordance with their spirit and plain intent, and that in such effort it has had to encounter and overcome difficulties and oppositions varied and intense in the extreme.

Early in the year, probably through the same subtle, elusive agency which in its last report (p. 79) the Bureau pointed out is constantly employed in the effort to make the labors of this service unavailing, rumors were circulated throughout this country and China that because of the effect produced upon public sentiment here by the use of the boycott there would be a general relaxation on the part of those charged with the enforcement of the Chinese exclusion laws, and that it would henceforth be a comparatively easy matter for the laborer to gain admission by assuming the guise of a member of the exempt classes. This erroneous impression, while apparently quite general, seems to have obtained particularly in the New England district; so that several of the most cunning and adept promoters of Chinese immigration located in and around that district, whose activities had been reduced to a minimum by the discouragement consequent upon the frustration of every plan which they had adopted during 1904–5, again entered the field. These promoters seem to have spread the report in China that the Canadian border ports would now be "open doors" for the introduction of coolies fortified with papers describing them as merchants returning to a former domicile in this country, or as the minor sons of merchants living here. The adoption of this plan was doubtless due to the promoters realizing that the instructions which, by the President's orders, had been issued to United States consular officers in the spring of 1905 (alluded to more particularly under subtitle 3 of this title, p. 83), would render it useless to again try the plan, that had once worked so successfully, of having laborers secure "section 6" certificates, describing them as merchants or students. At any rate, during the year a considerable number of laborers have presented themselves, principally at Port Townsend, Wash., and Richford, Vt., holding "affidavits" prepared in or near Boston, Mass., describing them as merchants or minor sons, which papers upon investigation have been found to be false, in some cases even the signatures and notary's seal being fictitious. It is believed, however, that all of these frauds were detected, and with the exception of a few cases still pending, the Chinamen have been returned to their native land. Thus it is that with the least, even imaginary, cause for encouragement, the promoter and smuggler reengage in their nefarious operations, abundance of material, in the shape of Chinese anxious to enter this to them paradise for labor, being always ready to their hands.

In appropriating for the expenses of enforcing the Chinese exclusion laws for the next fiscal year Congress has stipulated that the amount so authorized shall be drawn from the immigrant fund and not, as heretofore, from "moneys in the Treasury not otherwise appropriated." This having been done, the Bureau believes a further step should be taken—one which will actually attain the permanent and lasting benefits to be derived from considering the enforcement of the Chinese exclusion laws as a part of the duty devolving upon the officers charged with the administration of the general immigration laws, and therefore to be paid for out of the immigrant fund, which consists of the head tax collected upon aliens of all classes, including Chinese. When next appropriating for the payment of expenses of enforcing the Chinese exclusion laws it is thought that Congress should simply provide that thereafter such expenses shall be paid and accounted for in the same manner as those connected with the enforcement of the immigration laws proper, and that all officers employed in the Chinese branch of the service shall be designated and regarded as immigration officials. A real combination of the two branches would then be effected, with an incidental saving in time and labor connected with the handling of accounts, etc., and with the following results of incalculable benefit: (1) The abrogation of all distinction between immigrant and Chinese inspectors; (2) the general consolidation under one head (already accomplished to as great an extent as the separation of the two branches of the service permits) of the offices of inspectors in charge of immigration and Chinese matters in the different districts and at the various ports of the country; (3) the abolishment, to a considerable extent at least, of the quite general but wholly imaginary impression in the mind of the public that aliens of the Chinese race are treated, even allowing duly for the fact that the provisions of the law applying to them were purposely made more strict, with greater harshness and less consideration than those of other races; (4) a final effective step in the effort which the Bureau has exerted since being charged with the enforcement of the Chinese exclusion laws to produce a thorough cooperation and to eliminate all feeling of mutual jealousy between the officers of the two branches of the service—impediments to good administration which, when the Chinese inspectors were first placed under the Bureau, were quite marked, but which have now been considerably modified.

For the sake of convenience and clearness of presentation the further discussion of the subject is taken up under the subtitles into which it naturally falls in practice. The statistical tables are inserted and discussed in the next succeeding subtitle, and when referred to thereafter are mentioned by number.

2. Statistical Tables.

The tables relating to Chinese are designated by Arabic numerals to readily distinguish them from those concerning immigration proper.

Table 1 shows by classes the total number of Chinese cases handled (at seaports and border ports, respectively) during the fiscal year 1906, dividing those totals into cases pending from last year and new applications, and indicating how many of each were finally admitted and deported, respectively, and how many remained unsettled. At the bottom of said table a further segregation is given, so as to show the distribution of the cases between the different seaports and border ports.

Referring to Table 1 in the report for 1905 (pp. 81-82), it will be seen that the total number of cases handled during that year was 3,222; hence the past year's total, 3,015, is 207 less. It will also be noticed that at San Francisco during the past year 307 less cases were handled than in 1905, so that more than the entire loss occurred at that port, and there have been varying gains at several of the other ports, particularly Sumas, Malone, Richford, Boston, and New York. As to classes, a large gain has occurred in the alleged native applicant; the number of applications by alleged minor children of merchants has more than doubled; a considerable reduction is shown in the number of returning domiciled merchants and laborers, respectively, and in the class of exempts, exclusive of domiciled merchants and their wives and children, there has been a reduction from 898 in 1905 to 347 in 1906. The remarkable reduction in the "section 6" applicants is alluded to more particularly in subtitle 3 of this title (p. 83).

Table 1.—Chinese Seeking Admission to the United States, Fiscal Year 1906.

BORDER CASES.

Class.	Total cases.	New applications.	Pending from previous year.	Finally admitted.	Deported.	Pending close current year.
United States citizens	113	112	1	90	15	8
Wives of United States citizens	2	2		1		1
Returning laborers	75	69	6	75		
Returning merchants	170	164	6	145	14	11
Other merchants	36	36		36		
Merchants' wives	10	10		10		
Merchants' children	85	83	2	71	11	3
Students	18	18		14	1	3
Travelers	8	8		8		
Teachers	5	5		5		
Officials	2	2		2		
Miscellaneous						
Total	524	509	15	457	41	26

TABLE 1.—CHINESE SEEKING ADMISSION TO THE UNITED STATES, FISCAL YEAR 1906—Continued.

SEAPORT CASES.

Class.	Total cases.	New applications.	Pending from previous year.	Finally admitted.	Deported.	Pending close current year.
United States citizens	923	846	77	825	65	33
Wives of United States citizens	12	12		6		6
Returning laborers	375	365	10	356	18	1
Returning merchants	564	544	20	515	40	9
Other merchants	99	97	2	85	14	
Merchants' wives	37	37		36	1	
Merchants' children	298	286	12	274	22	2
Students	29	29		25	4	
Travelers	9	9		8		1
Teachers	7	7		7		
Officials	133	133		133		
Miscellaneous	5	5		5		
Total	2,491	2,370	121	2,275	164	52

TOTAL.

Class.	Total cases.	New applications.	Pending from previous year.	Finally admitted.	Deported.	Pending close current year.
United States citizens	1,036	958	78	915	80	41
Wives of United States citizens	14	14		7		7
Returning laborers	450	434	16	431	18	1
Returning merchants	734	708	26	660	54	20
Other merchants	135	133	2	121	14	
Merchants' wives	47	47		46	1	
Merchants' children	383	369	14	345	33	5
Students	47	47		39	5	3
Travelers	17	17		16		1
Teachers	12	12		12		
Officials	135	135		135		
Miscellaneous	5	5		5		
Grand total	3,015	2,879	136	2,732	205	78
In transit	611	611		605	5	1

BY PORTS.

Port.	Total cases.	New applications.	Pending from previous year.	Finally admitted.	Deported.	Pending close current year.
San Francisco, Cal	2,008	1,895	113	1,847	119	42
Port Townsend, Wash	221	213	8	187	24	10
Honolulu, Hawaii	199	199		193	6	
Sumas, Wash	203	193	10	189	8	6
Portal, N. Dak	54	54		50	2	2
Malone, N. Y	123	118	5	112	6	5
Richford, Vt	129	129		94	22	13
Boston, Mass	31	31		24	7	
New York, N. Y	24	24		21	3	
New Orleans, La	2	2		1	1	
Portland, Oreg	1	1		1		
El Paso, Tex	15	15		12	3	
San Diego, Cal	5	5		1	4	
Grand total	3,015	2,879	136	2,732	205	78

Table 2 is a restatement of the figures of the preceding table, but arranged so as to show by whom the Chinese were admitted and rejected, respectively, and before whom unsettled cases are pending; the same segregation also being followed regarding the various ports. Of the 2,732 Chinese admitted, 2,647 were landed by the administrative officers at the ports, 78 by the Department on appeal, and 7 by the courts; and of the 424 refused landing, 309 were rejected by the officers at the ports, 108 by the Department on appeal, and 7 by the courts.

TABLE 2.—CHINESE SEEKING ADMISSION TO THE UNITED STATES, FISCAL YEAR 1906.

Class.	Admissions.			Rejections.			Cases pending.			Cases finally disposed of.	
	By inspectors.	By Department.	By courts.	By inspectors.	By Department.	By courts.	Before inspectors.	Before Department.	Before courts.	Admitted.	Deported.
BORDER CASES.											
United States citizens	77	12	1	36	13	1	5	2	1	90	15
Wives of United States citizens		1					1			1	
Returning laborers	70	5		5						75	
Returning merchants	132	12	1	31	11		9	2		145	14
Other merchants	29	7		7						36	
Merchants' wives	10									10	
Merchants' children	67	2	2	14	9		3			71	11
Students	14				1		3			14	1
Travelers	8									8	
Teachers	5									5	
Officials	2									2	
Total	414	39	4	93	34	1	21	4	1	457	41
SEAPORT CASES.											
United States citizens	794	28	3	99	59	3	7	1	25	825	65
Wives of United States citizens	6			2	2				6	6	
Returning laborers	354	2		22	2		1			356	18
Returning merchants	512	3		46	3		6	3		515	40
Other merchants	85			13	3					85	14
Merchants' wives	36			1						36	1
Merchants' children	268	6		29	5	3	1	1		274	22
Students	25			4						25	4
Travelers	8						1			8	
Teachers	7									7	
Officials	133									133	
Miscellaneous	5									5	
Total	2,233	39	3	216	74	6	16	5	31	2,275	164
TOTAL.											
United States citizens	871	40	4	135	72	4	12	3	26	915	80
Wives of United States citizens	6	1		2	2		1		6	7	
Returning laborers	424	7		27	2		1			431	18
Returning merchants	644	15	1	77	14		15	5		660	54
Other merchants	114	7		20	3					121	14
Merchants' wives	46			1						46	1
Merchants' children	335	8	2	43	14	3	4	1		345	33
Students	39			4	1		3			39	5
Travelers	16						1			16	
Teachers	12									12	
Officials	135									135	
Miscellaneous	5									5	
Grand total	2,647	78	7	309	108	7	37	9	32	2,732	205
In transit	605			5			1			605	5
BY PORTS.											
San Francisco, Cal	1,808	36	3	165	55	2	7	4	31	1,847	119
Port Townsend, Wash	184	3		31	8		9	1		187	24
Honolulu, Hawaii	193			6	3					193	6
Sumas, Wash	169	20		29	5		5	1		189	8
Portal, N. Dak	44	6		9	2		1	1		50	2
Malone, N. Y	106	4	2	13	3	1	2	2	1	112	6
Richford, Vt	91	2	1	31	20		13			94	22
Boston, Mass	24			6	4	4				24	7
New York, N. Y	21			3	2					21	3
New Orleans, La	1			1						1	1
Portland, Oreg	1									1	
El Paso, Tex	4	7	1	11	4					12	3
San Diego, Cal	1			4	2					1	4
Grand total	2,647	78	7	309	108	7	37	9	32	2,732	205

TABLE 2.—CHINESE SEEKING ADMISSION TO THE UNITED STATES, FISCAL YEAR 1906—Continued.

SUMMARY.

Class.	Admitted.	Deported.	Class.	Admitted.	Deported.
United States citizens	915	80	Students	39	5
Wives of United States citizens	7		Travelers	10	
Returning laborers	431	18	Teachers	12	
Returning merchants	660	54	Officials	135	
Other merchants	121	14	Miscellaneous	5	
Members of merchants' families	391	34	Total	2,732	205

Of the 2,732 admitted, 1,985 were residents returning to the United States, and 747 were new arrivals. Of the 205 deported, 149 claimed to be residents and 56 new arrivals.

Of the total admissions and deportations, there were admitted at San Francisco 1,847, and deported from that port 119.

Table 3, showing action taken in the cases of Chinese arrested on the charge of being in the United States in violation of law, is compiled from statements furnished by the United States marshals. A similar table was published in the annual report for 1905 (pp. 89–90), to which reference can be made for comparative purposes if desired. It will be noted that of the number arrested during the past year, 503, those pending at the close of the previous year, 302, and those appealed by the Government from court order or discharged, 2 (aggregating 807), 10 died or escaped, 223 are still pending, 255 were discharged, and 319 were deported. The majority of the arrests made were of Chinese who had surreptitiously crossed the land boundaries; but few were taken into custody at interior points, and there have been no special searches instituted for those unlawfully here.

TABLE 3.—ACTION TAKEN IN THE CASES OF CHINESE PERSONS ARRESTED ON THE CHARGE OF BEING IN THE UNITED STATES IN VIOLATION OF LAW, DURING FISCAL YEAR ENDED JUNE 30, 1906.

Cases before United States commissioners.

Until order of deportation or discharge:		
Arrests		503
Pending before hearing at close of previous year		77
Total		580
Disposition:		
Died	1	
Escaped	1	
Forfeited bail	4	
Discharged	196	
Pending before hearing at close of present year	45	
Ordered deported	333	
After order of deportation:		
Ordered deported		333
Awaiting deportation or appeal at close of previous year		81
Total		414
Disposition:		
Deported	246	
Awaiting deportation or appeal to United States district courts at close of present year	48	
Appealed to United States district courts	120	

Cases before United States district courts.

Until order of deportation or discharge:		
Appealed to United States district courts		120
Pending before trial at close of previous year		108
Total		228
Disposition:		
Forfeited bail	1	
Discharged	58	
Pending before trial at close of present year	89	
Ordered deported	80	
After order of deportation:		
Ordered deported		80
Appealed by Government from court order of discharge		2
Awaiting deportation or appeal to higher courts at close of previous year		23
Total		105
Disposition:		
Escaped	3	
Deported	54	
Awaiting deportation or appeal at close of present year	3	
Appealed to higher courts	45	

Cases before higher United States courts.

Until order of deportation or discharge:		
Appealed to higher United States courts		45
Pending before trial at close of previous year		13
Total		58
Disposition:		
Discharged	1	
Pending before trial at close of present year	37	
Ordered deported	20	
After order of deportation:		
Ordered deported		20
Awaiting deportation at close of previous year		0
Total		20
Disposition:		
Deported	19	
Awaiting deportation	1	

Recapitulation of all cases.

Arrests		503
Appealed by Government from court order of discharge		2
Pending at close of previous year, including those awaiting deportation or appeal		302
Total		807
Disposition:		
Died, escaped, and forfeited bail	10	
Discharged	255	
Deported	319	
Pending at close of present year, including those awaiting deportation or appeal	223	

Table 4 (corresponding with an unnumbered one in last year's report, p. 85) covers the travel to and from China during the year of registered Chinese laborers. This subject is treated fully in subtitle 6 of this title (p. 86), and needs no special comment here.

TABLE 4.—ARRIVAL AND DEPARTURE OF REGISTERED CHINESE LABORERS DURING FISCAL YEAR ENDED JUNE 30, 1906.

Port.	Departure of laborers.	Return of laborers.	Port.	Departure of laborers.	Return of laborers.
San Francisco, Cal	499	226	Portal, N. Dak	33	10
Port Townsend, Wash	62	39	Malone, N. Y	98	11
Portland, Oreg	....	1	Richford, Vt	43	18
Honolulu, Hawaii	158	90			
Sumas, Wash	24	36	Total	917	431

Table 5 (printed at p. 96 of last year's report, unnumbered) shows, by ports, the number of Chinese cases in which appeals have been taken from excluding decisions rendered by officers in charge at ports of entry, and the action of the Department thereon.

TABLE 5.—APPEALS TO DEPARTMENT FROM EXCLUDING DECISIONS, UNDER CHINESE EXCLUSION LAWS, DURING FISCAL YEAR ENDED JUNE 30, 1906.

Action taken.	San Francisco, Cal.	Port Townsend, Wash.	Honolulu, Hawaii.	Sumas, Wash.	Portal, N. Dak.	Malone, N. Y.	Richford, Vt.	Boston, Mass.	New York, N. Y.	El Paso, Tex.	San Diego, Cal.	Total.
Pending at close of previous year	4	1	....	....	....	....	....	....	....	....	....	5
Appealed	105	11	3	27	9	9	27	9	2	12	2	216
Total	109	12	3	27	9	9	27	9	2	12	2	221
Disposition:												
Sustained (admitted)	36	3	....	20	6	4	2	....	....	7	....	78
Dismissed (rejected)	55	8	3	5	2	3	20	4	2	4	2	108
Withdrawn or disposed of by means other than departmental decision	14	....	....	1	....	....	3	5	....	1	....	24
Pending at close of current year	4	1	....	1	1	2	2	....	....	....	....	11

3. THE "SECTION 6" EXEMPT CLASSES.

In each report made by the present commissioner-general since his induction into office there has been pointed out in no uncertain terms the need for stationing in China representatives of this Department charged with the duty of investigating the cases of Chinese who secure from their Government the certificate prescribed by section 6 of the act approved July 5, 1884, such plan to supersede that of having the investigation made by United States consular officers. No legislation on the subject has yet been past by Congress. When in the spring of 1905 the agitation in China of the boycott of American goods became so persistent as to threaten our commercial relations with that country, the ground therefor being the claim that members of the exempt classes, although equipped with the evidence of their status required by law, were subjected to strict, time-consuming, and "humiliating" examination upon arrival at ports of this country, the President adopted a course which has resulted in greatly improved conditions. Under his orders consular officers abroad were instructed as to what their duties concerning these certificates are, and were informed that they would be held strictly to account for any failure to properly discharge them. Relying upon the effect of these emphatic orders, it has been possible for immigration officials at the ports of this country to accept the certificate upon a comparison of it with the applicant and a sufficient examination of the latter to insure his identity with the person described therein, and at the same time to feel reasonably sure that no fraud was being imposed upon the Government. That in the past the certificate was often issued and viséed in a wholly perfunctory if not intentionally fraudulent manner is shown conclusively by the number of applicants that by close examination the officers were able to detect as frauds, and receives further confirmation in the great reduction in the number of applicants of this class reaching the United States since the promulgation of the President's orders and in the number rejected. In 1904, 514 Chinese arrived from China claiming to be members of the exempt classes, of whom 35 were rejected; in 1905, 898 applied, of whom 257 were rejected; and in the past fiscal year only 328 (a large proportion, 135 being officials) have presented themselves, of whom 19 have been deported, not in every instance, however, because fraud was shown, but in a number of cases under section 2 of the immigration act approved March 3, 1903, the applicants being found afflicted with a dangerous contagious disease. In other words, in 1905 it was necessary to reject about 29 per cent of the exempts arriving from China, whereas in 1906 less than 6 per cent were refused admission. Moreover, it has been possible to arrange with the Department of State a system by which the Bureau promptly receives reports regarding the visé of section 6 certificates by the several consular officers in China, and is enabled to advise the officials at the ports where the holders of such certificates propose to enter, and to conduct, pending the arrival of the applicant, investigations in this country in the rare cases susceptible of such action, in which manner several attempted frauds have been detected during the year. The officials of the two Departments are thus cooperating with each other to the greatest extent possible; the consular officers are learning more about the exclusion laws and are regarding their duties more seriously than heretofore, and the immigration officials are in turn able to accord more weight to the certificates without the feeling, amounting almost to conviction, which they formerly had, that they were being deceived by the Chinese and that the visé of the consul meant nothing more than a perfunctory signing of his name.

The immigration officers have always been just as willing and anxious to admit members of the exempt as to debar members of the excluded classes. The personal appearance of the Chinamen who were applying, and their poverty and ignorance, were too palpable evidence of the fraudulent character of their claims that they were merchants, students, teachers, or travelers to permit of any other course by the inspectors than to avail themselves of the only feasible plan by which to "controvert" the certificate, as provided by Congress itself, namely, the oral examination of each applicant concerning the details covered by his certificate and his knowledge of the claimed pursuit. That this course was a correct one is demonstrated by the result—the debarment from this country in the two years, 1904 and 1905, of 292 Chinese of the class which it is the avowed desire of the Governments of both this country and of China to exclude. In many cases, however, efforts of immigration officers were not successful, and it is believed that a most conservative estimate is that of the 1,448 Chinese admitted as members of the exempt classes during the said years one-half were common laborers or coolies.

The Bureau wishes that it could express the opinion that the serious problem of properly guarding the country from the entrance thereto of the excluded classes, and at the same time of insuring the making of no mistake and the giving of no offense in the continuous effort to receive the real merchant, student, and teacher courteously and hospitably, has been permanently and satisfactorily solved. But it can not. With the added experience of another year it is more than ever convinced that the only proper method of enforcing this law consists in a discontinuance of the present system of divided responsibility, and the stationing in China of immigration officers directly under its control. The inconsistency and impropriety of requiring of a consular officer, who is placed at his station for the paramount purpose of encouraging commerce, no small part of which duty consists in cultivating friendly relations with the people and their officials, to pursue a line of inquiry which necessarily in many instances involves what must be regarded as a close scrutiny of, or perhaps a suspicious attitude toward, the acts of such Chinese officials, are too obvious to require elucidation. The difficulties and embarrassments of this condition are alluded to in several dispatches from consular officers, copies of which have been received by the Bureau from the State Department, and some specific cases have come to the Bureau's attention during the past year illustrating this, and also the fact that efforts are still made with varying success to deceive the consular officers. These dispatches furnish strong corroboration of the view that a perfect arrangement of this matter requires that the investigations shall be made by officers of the Bureau of Immigration versed in the practical application of the law, and charged with no responsibilities at variance with a proficient performance of the duty, and answerable directly to the Department of Commerce and Labor.

A plan for taking up at ports of entry "section 6" certificates presented by members of the exempt classes and issuing to them cards of identification for their future protection is discussed under subtitle 8 of this title (p. 88).

4. The Domiciled Merchant.

Table 1 (p. 78) shows that during the year 145 domiciled merchants have after temporary visits abroad reentered the country. With the perfect plan employed for identifying members of said class the frauds by which laborers were formerly introduced under this guise have been discouraged; and, while such frauds are still frequently attempted, it is believed that they are promptly detected in most if not all instances. The guise is still employed quite extensively, with varying success, for the purpose of enabling laborers, not registered and therefore not able to avail themselves of either the legitimate or the illegitimate route employed by the registered laborer, to visit China and effect a safe reentry. This deception is frequently detected, but doubtless, by reason of its cunning and clever inception and performance, quite as frequently escapes detection. The best that can be done is to carefully, but courteously, examine the applicants and their witnesses and to closely scrutinize the evidence for indications of perjury. By such means 14 alleged merchants were found not to belong to that class and were deported.

The advantages which would accrue, if another registration is attempted, of specifying that a certificate of residence will thereafter be the only admissible evidence, aside from the pursuit in which a Chinaman is found engaged, to show lawfulness of residence, are pointed out under subtitle 7 of this title (p. 87).

5. Wives and Minor Childern of Domiciled Merchants.

This is a class the admission of which has to be carefully guarded, because the guise of wife or minor daughter is so easily availed of when some one of the numerous secret societies desires to import a prostitute or slave girl, and that of the minor son can be employed to an unlimited extent for introducing young laborers. The attempts in both of these respects have been numerous during the past year, but it is hoped that the majority at least of the 46 "wives" and 345 "minor children" shown by Table 1 (p. 78) to have been admitted as members of this class have been the actual wives and minor children of real merchants. One resultant evil, however, it seems impossible to obviate. In many instances the minor sons, admitted solely because of the membership of their fathers in the exempt class, are scarcely in the country before they engage in laboring pursuits. Thus the number of laborers in this country is increased by a means unforeseen and not provided against, and it is extremely difficult to obtain from the courts orders for the deportation of such laborers when they show that they have been regularly admitted by administrative officers. With a view to prevent any possibility of doubt on this point, a provision should be incorporated in the law to the effect that minor children may be admitted only for the purpose of joining their fathers and engaging in exempt pursuits and if found later employed as laborers shall be arrested and deported. The Bureau can see no other way of closing this loophole.

6. The Domiciled Laborer.

Table 4 (p. 83) shows that during the year 917 laborers left this country for China with the avowed intention of returning, and that 431 such laborers were readmitted after temporary absence. These figures, of course, cover only the cases of those laborers who have made application to immigration officers for the return certificate required by sections 5, 6, and 7 of the act of September 13, 1888, and who were able to meet the conditions of said sections. The provisions of this statute are difficult of performance, and it is known that many domiciled laborers, rather than attempt to meet them, prefer to simply secrete their residence certificate on their person and proceed abroad, taking the chance of being successful in an endeavor to later cross the Mexican border without detection and then, if accosted by an inspector, produce the certificate and deny having been out of the United States. As an illustration of this, it appears from a report of the inspector in charge, El Paso, Tex., dated January 25, 1906, that at that point alone there had crossed the border during the preceding six months 250 Chinese of this class. These laborers, being in possession of certificates of residence, it would have been worse than useless to arrest them, as the court commissioner at El Paso would not order the deportation of such Chinese in the absence of affirmative proof that they had been out of the United States. Moreover, it is confidently believed that the majority of such Chinamen as attempt to comply with these provisions present fictitious cases supported by perjured testimony, the condition usually selected by them—that concerning the existence of debts aggregating $1,000—being one concerning which a plausible story can without great difficulty be agreed upon between several witnesses with slight chance of detection. The Bureau does not hesitate to say, therefore, that these provisions of the law are incapable of enforcement in that efficient degree that should be attained by administrative officers in carrying out the will of the people as expressed by Congress, and that they tend to encourage perjury, deceit, and smuggling—the latter because the fact that Chinese of this class enter clandestinely with impunity leads the new coolie from China to believe that he can also do so. Thus a situation on the Mexican border, sufficiently deplorable otherwise (as shown under subtitle 12 of this title, p. 93), is rendered all the more difficult to handle. But beyond this, in their practical application these provisions have an effect the opposite of that intended by their framers; for their unnecessarily exacting terms, instead of tending to reduce the number of laborers here, discourage them from leaving, and then proceed to state that unless such laborers return within one year, or at the most two, they shall be denied readmission, thus causing many of the very class that it is the avowed intention and desire to exclude, or to reduce in numbers, to return and take up their residence here, when, if not so restricted, they might remain out of the country for long terms of years or permanently. The Bureau is impelled therefore to recommend that these provisions be amended so as to permit lawfully resident laborers to depart and return with no further restrictions than that they shall deposit at the port of departure, for identification purposes upon their return to the same port at any future time, their certificate of residence. Besides producing the effects already enumerated, this would materially simplify and reduce the cost of administering the law.

7. Proposed Registration of Chinese.

Notwithstanding the difficulties that would necessarily attach to the performance of the labor incident to conducting another registration of Chinese, it is thought that the Bureau should be authorized to undertake it. Of course, one result would be the legalizing of the residence here of hundreds, or perhaps thousands, of Chinese laborers who have been smuggled in since the date of the last registration act, November 3, 1893. But many advantages would accrue therefrom. With the experience gained during the time the Bureau has had in charge the enforcement of the exclusion laws, and by the employment of its corps of able and experienced officers, a registration could be made that would be both complete and efficacious. A certificate could be devised that it would be extremely difficult if not impossible to counterfeit, and the record of the registration could be arranged so as to be absolutely trustworthy for future reference. A law contemplating such registration should require, with proper penalties for failure, that all laborers resident in the United States on a certain recent date, irrespective of whether or not they were registered under prior acts, shall appear before immigration officials, establish their residence here on such date, and receive a certificate. It should also grant to all persons of the Chinese race who claim birth in the United States the privilege of securing such a certificate upon proving the claim before an immigration official designated to issue the certificates, thus insuring to the Chinese-American citizen a means of protecting himself against the presumption necessarily created by his belonging to that race and saving the Government much trouble and expense in the future handling of such cases. Members of the exempt classes domiciled here should also be accorded the privilege; for, while perhaps it would not be expedient to require them to register, they should not be left without a measure for their protection should they afterwards by stress of misfortune become laborers. In this respect, however, what the Bureau believes must certainly have been the intent of Congress in the registration acts of 1892 and 1893, viz, that the possession of a certificate of residence would be the only evidence permissible at a later date to show the lawfulness of the residence here during the registration period of a member of the exempt classes who had become a laborer, should be stated in plain, unmistakable terms. Thus would be avoided a repetition of the experience that so many laborers now here without a certificate claim, when arrested, that they were merchants during the registration period and were not therefore required to register; for such a laborer would immediately be called upon to produce the only admissible evidence to substantiate his claim, i. e., a certificate issued to him as an exempt.

In addition to the foregoing, provision should be made in connection with any scheme to hold another registration that, after the expiration of one year from the date of the registration act, any Chinese laborer found in the United States who has not a residence certificate shall be taken into custody by immigration officials, on a Department warrant, and, after hearing before administrative officers and a finding by such officers that he is here unlawfully, be deported. This would furnish an economical and thoroughly efficient means for handling such cases and would avoid a recurrence of the unfortunate and costly experience—a description of which has occupied much space in former reports of the Bureau—that has resulted from the present method of having judicial hearings, mostly before United States commissioners, in all cases of Chinese arrested for unlawful residence. If any objection is urged to transferring this function from the judicial to the administrative branch of the Government, the reply is the fact that such authority is already possessed by the latter branch concerning all aliens except Chinese, and that no undesirable but, on the contrary, the most beneficial, results have attended the exercise of such authority by the administrative officers.

8. Proposed Issuance of Certificates of Identification to Admitted Members of the Exempt Classes.

Another question, analogous to that covered by the last subtitle and of equal importance, is the adoption of a suitable plan for the prompt, sure, and convenient identification of Chinese of the exempt classes when traveling from point to point in the United States at any time subsequent to admission at a port of entry. Until recently the practice was followed of taking up and placing on file at the ports of entry the certificates presented by Chinese admitted as members of the exempt classes. This procedure resulted in some complaint, it being contended that the clause in the law requiring that such certificate should be "afterward (after the admission of the holder) produced to the proper authorities of the United States whenever lawfully demanded" indicated an intention upon the part of Congress that such certificate should be returned to and carried on the person of the Chinaman. While this view is, the Bureau believes, erroneous (for the certificate can be quite as readily and much more surely produced from the files of the office at the port than from the person of the Chinaman), the rules of the Department have been amended to require that such papers be returned to applicants, as was done prior to the time that the enforcement of the exclusion laws was vested in the Bureau. This results in a return to the old conditions, under which it was possible to carry on an extensive traffic in these "section 6" certificates, such papers being of a character easily forged and altered. Moreover, because of the bulk and texture of these certificates, they can not long be kept in a legible condition, and after being carried in the pocket of the holder for a while become worthless for purposes of identification. The Bureau desires therefore to again urge the importance of issuing in lieu of the "section 6" certificate, which in its opinion should in every instance be taken up when presented, such a certificate of identification as is described in Rule 59 of the regulations approved May 3, 1905, which rule was never put into operation and was omitted from the regulations approved February 5, 1906. The object of that rule was to place in the hands of every Chinese merchant, student, teacher, or traveler lawfully admitted to this country a durable card of suitable size for carrying in the pocket without folding or bending, as handsomely engraved as a bank note and as difficult to counterfeit, thus providing a convenient and sure means of identifying such person at any and all times and places within the United States, avoiding by the attachment of photographs to the cards the possibility of transferring them to persons not entitled thereto. It is believed that both the prevention of frauds against the Government and the proper protection of the members of the exempt classes when absent from the places at which they pursue their vocations—the engagement of such Chinese in their lawful pursuits being their usual and permanent means of protection—demand that a plan substantially like that outlined in the said abandoned rule shall be inaugurated, either by readopting the rule or through legislation on the subject—the former if the Department agrees with the construction placed upon the law by the Bureau and the latter if it does not.

If all Chinese now in this country are effectively registered and the deportation of those afterwards found unlawfully here placed in the hands of the administrative branch of the Government, as suggested in the preceding subtitle, and provision made for a proper method of identifying those later admitted as members of the exempt classes, the Bureau believes that the way will have been prepared for a much more thorough, just, and satisfactory enforcement of the exclusion policy than is possible under the somewhat anomalous conditions now existing.

9. The "Native Born."

Attention is particularly invited to the figures contained in Table 2 (p. 80) showing that during the year 911 Chinese have been admitted by administrative officers as American citizens by birth, and to Table 3 (p. 81), from which it appears that the courts during the same time have discharged 255 persons of said race, many of whom were discharged as citizens by birth. Thus the "inestimable heritage" is conferred upon persons belonging to a race that Congress has declared shall not be admitted to citizenship by naturalization, and it is safe to say that the vast majority of those thus invested are utterly ignorant and careless, not only of our institutions and ideas, but of the very language of the country in which they claim to have been born. Those admitted by administrative officers are principally "returning natives"—that is to say, they are Chinamen who have lived in this country for varying periods, and who have visited China, usually for the purpose of being married and of establishing a family in the "native village" of their forefathers. These "natives" submit conclusive evidence of having lived in the United States and as a rule the fairly consistent testimony of two or more clansmen to the effect that they were born here. While the admission of these Chinamen, who are with rare exception laborers or coolies, does not add to the Chinese population, it places them in a position to claim in the future all the privileges of American citizens, including the visiting at will of their wives in China, and the assertion whenever they choose in the future of the right to bring here their foreign-born and foreign-reared families. When the subject is viewed in its broad significance, the Bureau believes the immigration officials would not be properly performing their duty by doing less than to require quite convincing proofs from this class of persons, especially as usually the very circumstances preclude the possibility of the Government's proving a negative. On the other hand, those members of this class who have been declared citizens by the courts and court commissioners have consisted largely of Chinamen who walk across the border line of Mexico or Canada and upon being arrested claim that they were born in the United States and when children were taken or sent to China by their parents. Realizing that, under the efficient plan to prevent coaching and the expeditious manner in which cases are handled by administrative officers at ports, their chances of gaining entry by regular means are meager, the members of this class, belonging almost exclusively to the coolie or the lowest caste of China, adopt the plan above mentioned whereby delay and the incidental opportunity for presenting a fictitious case are assured them.

The menace to a continuance of our policy of excluding Chinese laborers presented by the so-called "native-born" overshadows every other, and is the problem of chief importance now confronting the efficient enforcement of the laws. As the years pass it will doubtless increase; for soon we will be receiving at our doors the children born of Chinese mothers, and reared in China according to the Chinese usages and customs, of Chinamen who have lived for a number of years in this country and who have claimed and been invested with citizenship. How can we best meet this menace and provide against its future growth? It is believed the only measure that will prove even fairly effective is that suggested under subtitle 7 of this title

(p. 87), viz, to permit those who claim such citizenship to register as natives upon proving their claim, and to place in administrative hands the duty of arresting and trying Chinese laborers found here without certificates.

During the early months of the year indications were developed of an extensive revival of the importation of slave girls and prostitutes. The claim that these girls and women are the daughters and wives of domiciled merchants has been employed to some extent, but the favorite method has consisted in having such females marry young Chinamen, whose native birth has been declared by the courts or administrative officers, thus giving them the status of wives of American citizens. In a number of cases conclusive proof of the claimed marriage, in the form of marriage certificates of undoubted authority, were furnished, and no other course was possible than to land the girls. By keeping them and their alleged husbands under surveillance, it was found that they were placed in Chinese houses of ill fame, apparently being disposed of to the highest bidder. In other instances it was possible, by a rigid cross-examination of the women and their alleged husbands, to develop evidence sufficient to establish that, if a ceremony were performed at all, it was a mere mock marriage adopted for the purpose of defeating the exclusion laws, or that the man was already married to another woman before his so-called marriage to the applicant had occurred. Thus it has been possible to deport some of these women to the country whence they came. A large party of these prostitutes was brought to Mexico on one occasion, being carried through Canada in transit and then to Veracruz by steamer. In Mexico they were met by young Chinese from this country and ceremonies of marriage were performed before Mexican civil justices, by whom marriage certificates under seal were issued. Several of these couples presented themselves at El Paso, Tex., demanding the right to cross the border by reason of the American citizenship of the husbands. One of the said couples, in whose case the strongest evidence of the parties' good faith was furnished, on appealing to the Department, was permitted to land. An efficient officer was detailed to follow them to whatever point they might proceed and ascertain what was done with the girl. The couple immediately boarded a train for San Francisco, and upon arrival there the girl was taken to a boarding house on Dupont street, near one of the alleys of Chinatown's prostitute section. Negotiations were then quite apparently opened with the proprietors of the leading brothels; for the "husband" was observed to proceed from time to time to these different houses, returning accompanied by the respective proprietors. Before the bids were all in and the human merchandise "knocked down" to the highest bidder, however, San Francisco was visited by the earthquake, which obliterated all trace of this and doubtless of many another similar crime. A timely holding by the Department that, while the marriage of a Chinese woman to a Chinese-American citizen entitles her to the privilege of entering this country to reside with her husband, such marriage does not change her status as a person of the Chinese race and does not give her the right to enter at any other than the regularly designated ports of entry for Chinese, has resulted in forcing this class of applicants to abandon the Mexican border ports and proceed to San Francisco, or some other regular port of entry, where the facilities for sifting the evidence presented and establishing the fraudulent character of the cases are much better than elsewhere; and the San Francisco earthquake has, doubtless only temporarily, disconcerted the plans of some of the importers. Thus is the boon of American citizenship, often so carelessly and inconsiderately conferred upon the Chinese resident, prostituted to the accomplishment of results so utterly at variance with American civilization and so repugnant to every moral sensibility of our Christian nation.

10. The Transit.

Table 1 (p. 78) shows that 605 Chinese have passed through the United States in transit to other countries. With regard to these transits all of the details of a complete system of bonding, recording, and identifying them have been observed by the careful employees charged with the important duty. There is no reason for changing the opinion heretofore expressed that many who proceed to Mexico, the West Indies, and Central America do so with the ultimate intention of smuggling into the United States.

The transit Chinese belong to one of two classes: (1) Those who are exempted from the excluding provisions of the law on condition that they present a certificate showing their status as merchants, teachers, students, or travelers, and (2) *all others*. The first, if they present the certificate required by the *mandatory terms* of section 6 of the act of July 5, 1884, are admitted promptly upon arrival and identification and may then remain in or proceed through the United States at will. The second are permitted to pass through the United States under departmental regulations (there being no direct authority of law by which their transit could be allowed), which regulations have existed for years and have been emphatically approved by the Supreme Court of the United States (Fok Yung Yo *v.* United States, 185 U. S., 296). Failure upon the part of the Chinese and those interested in them to observe this perfectly plain distinction has occasionally produced misunderstanding and embarrassment, resulting in unwarranted criticism of administrative officers, who are always anxious to extend courtesies and accommodations to those Chinese who belong to the exempt classes. It can be confidently stated that even in the very rare instances in which trouble has been experienced all delay or other difficulty could have been avoided by the exercise of a little forethought and care on the part of the Chinese or those interested in them to observe the simple provisions of the law, with which such persons should be familiar or could readily acquaint themselves.

11. The Chinese Seaman.

As Chinese labor can be secured at a lower wage than any other, and as the members of that race make fair sailors, many of the vessels that come to our ports—from the magnificent trans-Pacific liner down to the small sailing ship—employ them as members of their crews. In view of the exclusion laws, the seamen can not be permitted to land except under the strictest of regulations to insure their departure. During the year it has been necessary to guard against the landing of over 16,000 such aliens, an undertaking of considerable magnitude. The law provides a penalty against any master who allows a Chinaman to escape into the United States, and in some instances it has been possible to secure convictions, with salutary results of value. But at some of the most important ports the courts have, "in the interest of commerce," or because of the failure of the Government to show affirmatively connivance by the master in the escape, dealt so leniently with the ship captains charged with this offense that administrative officers experience much difficulty in preventing the landing of these laborers.

The inspector in charge at the port of New York, where the above-mentioned condition is particularly trying, suggests in his annual report to the Bureau that the law should be so amended as to attach a definitely fixed, severe penalty to the permitting of a landing, even though there is no actual connivance on the part of the master, and a more severe penalty when such connivance is shown. This suggestion meets with the unqualified approval of the Bureau, for experience has demonstrated the need of adopting more drastic measures of protection in this regard; and, certainly, if the masters and owners of vessels, for reasons of economy and gain, insist on bringing into our ports large bodies of coolie seamen, they should be compelled to observe every precaution to prevent their entering this country contrary to law.

In this connection attention is directed to the remarks contained in the last annual report of the Bureau (p. 100) and in the report for 1904 (pp. 148–149). It is highly important to an enforcement of both the Chinese exclusion and the alien contract-labor laws that some legislation shall be had that will definitely settle the existing anomalous condition that, when it is to the advantage of the Chinaman and his employer to so hold, the deck of a vessel of American register is regarded as American soil, but when it would be to the interest of a proper administration of the Chinese exclusion and alien contract-labor laws to so hold, i. e., in cases where Chinese are employed as seamen on board of vessels of American register plying to American ports, the condition of the law, as explained in said reports, is such that the hands of the executive branch of the Government are practically tied. All doubt on the subject of how the deck of an American vessel should be regarded in connection with the various features of these laws should be removed by Congress, in the interest both of good administration and of that portion of our own labor that engages in seafaring pursuits, which under present conditions does not receive the same measure of protection as labor employed in vocations followed on land.

12. Canadian and Mexican Border Conditions.

In several former reports of the Bureau it was necessary to refer at length to the deplorable conditions regarding the smuggling of Chinese existing on the Canadian border. It is gratifying in the extreme to be able now to say that those difficulties are believed to be things of the past. The highly satisfactory manner in which the Canadian Pacific Railway officials have observed the letter and spirit of the agreement entered into on February 23, 1903 (a copy of which may be found in the report for that year, p. 100), the hearty cooperation of the Department of Justice in the prosecution of smugglers and smuggled Chinese, and in contending in the courts for a construction of the law that would leave in the control of the administrative officers the decision of questions of citizenship raised regarding aliens brought to the boundary seeking admission, and the decision of the Supreme Court on this subject in the widely discussed and much misunderstood Ju Toy case, together with the cordial spirit of friendship for us and our exclusion policy exhibited on all occasions by the Canadian immigration officials, have all combined to produce this pleasing result.

On the Canada-New York border 102 Chinese were arrested and tried after having surreptitiously crossed into the United States, of whom 82 were released by United States commissioners as American citizens, 2 being deported, and 18 cases remaining unsettled at the close of the year. Many of these Chinese were brought from China and carried through Canada in bond to Newfoundland, from which point they were shipped over a railroad not controlled by the Canadian Pacific Railway Company to the northern New York border, where they crossed into the United States and were arrested. As soon as this fact was discovered it was reported to the controller of Chinese for Canada, and instructions were promptly issued that no more Chinese should be bonded through Canada to points on the border other than regular ports of entry. The importance of this order, the result of which is to compel all Chinese seeking to enter through Canada to submit to an examination as to their citizenship by the regularly constituted immigration authorities of the United States, under reasonable restrictions to prevent coaching and the introduction of perjured testimony, is well illustrated by the outcome of the 102 cases above mentioned.

The Bureau only wishes that something half so encouraging as the above could be said with regard to the Mexican border. But it has not been possible to arrange any such plan of cooperation there; and, although the efficiency of the service along that border has been materially improved and the lines have been drawn closer, a more strict guard of the usual routes of travel being maintained, the forces and devices of the smugglers and the number of candidates for surreptitious entry have been correspondingly increased. There can be but one conclusion drawn from the fact that large numbers of Chinese coolies are constantly arriving in those sections of Mexico that lie immediately contiguous to the border line—where there is no need for their services—and the fact that the Chinese population of said sections does not increase, to wit, that by some means they are smuggled into this country and conveyed to interior points. The inspector in charge of the district of Texas, with headquarters at El Paso, reports that during the year 516 Chinese laborers arrived in Juarez, Mexico (opposite El Paso), of whom only 5 returned to the interior of Mexico, leaving 511 to be smuggled into the United States. Several instances of smuggling by the carload have been detected, and one party in a gasoline sloop was captured on the southern California coast, but doubtless most of the smuggling is done on a smaller scale. Reference is made elsewhere in this report (subtitle 6 of this title, p. 86), to the manner and the extent of smuggling registered Chinese laborers across the Mexican border, and how their success further complicates an already unbearable condition, and a remedy is suggested for that particular feature of the evil.

Unless the plan described in subtitle 7 of this title (p. 87) for the registration of all Chinese now here and the inauguration at the same time, with regard to the arrest, trial, and deportation of Chinese, of the methods now so successfully employed concerning aliens of other races who gain admission unlawfully, or some means is found of securing the cooperation of all concerned on the Mexican, as is now done on the Canadian, border (of which no hope can now be held out), the smuggling of Chinese from Mexico can only be effectually curbed by maintaining a much closer patrol, night and day, than is possible with the force at present employed, supplementing such patrol by a very vigorous policy with regard to the arrest of Chinese found in this country in violation of law, so as to let it be known that even thickly settled city districts will not afford, as in the past, a fairly safe harbor for those who clandestinely enter. The equally difficult and discouraging question of controlling the Mexican border situation with regard to other aliens is discussed under subtitle 6 of Title I (p. 68).

Another disagreeable circumstance that is constantly being encountered, particularly on the Mexican border, consists of the cunning manner in which Chinese living in foreign contiguous territory, who desire to visit their relatives and friends in China, avail themselves of our exclusion laws to accomplish their purpose at the expense of this Government. Such a Chinaman will surreptitiously cross the line and conceal himself for a short while, and then manage, always with the exercise of more or less caution to prevent arousing suspicion concerning his real motive, to place himself in the way of being arrested and brought to trial on the charge of unlawful residence in the United States. He knows that he will be comfortably housed and fed pending the hearing of his case and that in the event of his deportation no cruelty or hardship will be visited upon him, and is therefore quite as willing to travel to the coast and across the Pacific as a prisoner as in the capacity of an ordinary steerage passenger. Of course, if such a person is caught in the act of crossing the border he is merely turned back and his purpose is frustrated. But if successful in crossing and concealing himself, there is no means available by which to establish the fact, denied by him, that he actually lived in the foreign country from which the immigration officers may feel morally certain he entered the United States. Consequently the order of the court for his deportation reads "to China," the country which, for reasons of his own, he is anxious to visit. Numerous cases of the character mentioned have arisen during the period covered by this report, but one is a particularly striking illustration of this practice by which the Chinaman turns the exclusion laws to his own profit. At El Paso there was "found concealed in Chinatown" an aged Chinese leper, who was immediately recognized by the officers as a person who, like the lepers described in Scripture, had been for a year past "begging by the wayside" in Juarez, Mexico. His clansmen in Mexico had tired of this burden upon their charity, and had smuggled him across, thinking thus to economically shift the responsibility for his care onto the shoulders of other clansmen in China by securing an order for his deportation from the United States to his native country. A delegation of the residents of Chinatown, El Paso, called upon the inspector in charge and signified their desire to testify against the leper. Upon finding that said official was indisposed to help them by bringing the Chinaman to trial, they took up a subscription among themselves, amounting to $45, which they presented to the leper, placed him on a car bound for Juarez, and notified him that if he ever reentered the United States he would be assassinated. Upon reaching Juarez his countrymen there refused to have anything more to do with him, and at last accounts he was isolated in the Juarez public hospital. While perhaps no plan could be devised that would effectively prevent this species of imposition, it is believed that placing the arrest and trial of Chinese in the exclusive control of administrative officers, as recommended under subtitle 7 of this title, would tend to its discouragement and perhaps eventually result in its discontinuance.

13. Reports of Inspectors in Charge.

When this Bureau and the Immigration Service became a part of the Department of Commerce and Labor it was necessary, in the interest of an economical, efficient, and satisfactory enforcement of the exclusion laws, to divide the territory of the United States into districts of convenient size. Officers of experience and tried integrity were placed in charge of these several districts and it is those officials and those in charge at ports of entry for Chinese that are referred to constantly as "inspectors in charge." The Bureau is in close touch with these officers at all times, and at the end of each year receives reports from them containing reviews and summaries of the work accomplished. If space permitted, those reports would be extensively quoted, for they are replete with data and ideas of value to a proper understanding of the subject of Chinese exclusion. But the Bureau must content itself with a short reference to some of the more important.

From the commissioner of immigration at San Francisco information is received to the effect that satisfactory, and in some respects remarkable, progress has been made in his district (the State of California) in the enforcement of the Chinese exclusion laws, especially concerning the detection and apprehension of smuggled Chinese and those engaged in smuggling them on the southern border; that the actual amount of work accomplished at the port of San Francisco, notwithstanding the falling off in entries of Chinese occasioned by the earthquake, has exceeded that of any preceding year; that his corps of efficient employees has been more successful than ever in detecting frauds attempted by those interested in the promotion of Chinese immigration, and that he believes attempts to perpetrate fraud have been less frequent than in the past, largely because of the good effect produced by the orders issued in the spring of 1905 to consular officers in China.

The inspector in charge of the district of Oregon states that the enforcement of the laws in his district and at the port of Portland has proceeded evenly and uneventfully, despite the fact that the Chinese population has been considerably augmented since the San Francisco earthquake; that only a very few arrests of Chinese unlawfully in the country have been made, as the courts and commissioners have been exceedingly busy with the land-fraud cases; and that both his office and the Bureau are to be felicitated upon the fact that the successful manner in which the Chinese who attended the Louisiana Purchase Exposition at St. Louis were handled, resulting in the defeat of the extensive plans to make use of the fair as a means of permanently introducing laborers (see pp. 90–92 of the Annual Report for 1905), prevented the repetition of such attempt in connection with the Lewis and Clark Exposition held at Portland.

The inspectors in charge of the district of Washington and of the two ports of entry located therein—Port Townsend and Sumas—submit reports showing that the large volume of business that has fallen to them in connection with the enforcement of the laws has been transacted promptly and thoroughly and with satisfaction to all except those who are opposed to the exclusion policy.

The business of the New England district and the ports of entry for Chinese located therein—Boston and Richford—is conducted under a joint arrangement, the commissioner of immigration at Boston being in charge of the said district and of the port of Boston and the inspector in charge at Richford, besides his duties in that capacity, acting as assistant to the commissioner at Boston and throughout New England. Letters received from these two officers show that much activity has prevailed in their district during the year, and that, perhaps with the exception of the Mexican border, it has been the scene of more attempts to import and smuggle Chinese coolies than any other section of the country. These various bold and cunning efforts of the promoters have been met by the skill which is gained from long experience with the Chinese and the smuggler and their methods, and it is thought that the year has been anything but a profitable one for those engaged in the business of importing Chinese laborers.

In the New York district also there are two ports of entry, New York City and Malone. The latter has in the past been one of the favorite ports for the introduction of Chinese laborers, the claim of American birth being the one most frequently employed, and the New York-Canadian border has been an active field of operations for the smugglers. The inspector in charge of this important district and its two ports therefore congratulates the Bureau upon the vastly improved conditions, brought about by the agreement with the Canadian Pacific Railway and the decisions of the Supreme Court regarding the authority of administrative officers to decide questions of citizenship raised in connection with applications to enter this country made by persons apparently aliens. Such Chinese as now come to the New York border are presented at Malone for examination by the inspectors, and, with the exception of the few mentioned under subtitle 12 of this title (p. 94), no smuggling has occurred.

Reports received from the commissioner of immigration at Philadelphia, in charge of the district of Pennsylvania, New Jersey, and Delaware, and from the inspectors in charge of the other Atlantic coast districts, and of the several districts into which the Middle and Rocky Mountain States are divided, and the port of entry of Portal, N. Dak., while reciting the occurrence of nothing striking or of paramount importance, indicate that the provisions of law concerning exclusion have received the usual close attention.

New Orleans was until recently a point at which the unlawful landing of Chinese was accomplished on an extensive scale. The

Bureau is therefore much gratified to be able to refer to the report of the inspector in charge at said city, who also exercises jurisdiction over the district of Louisiana and Mississippi, to the effect that the care and caution that have been exercised have resulted in the practical abandonment of the port by the promoter and smuggler.

As stated under the preceding subtitle, the Mexican border now constitutes the most feasible and prolific field for the operations of the smuggler. Three districts lie along that border, viz, the Texas district, the New Mexico-Arizona district, and the California district. The California border is under the direct supervision of a capable, energetic officer, subordinate to the commissioner at San Francisco, and has already been mentioned. From the inspectors in charge of the other two, whose headquarters are located at El Paso and Tucson, respectively, valuable reports have been received. Considering the facilities and the size of the corps of officers at their command, as compared with the difficulties, natural and artificial, to be overcome, the results accomplished are remarkable. Much remains to be desired. In fact it is extremely doubtful whether the Mexican border problem will be solved with entire satisfaction until some radical change from the present system of enforcing the law is made, but that the best possible under existing circumstances is being done by the conscientious officials charged with the difficult duty of guarding the long border line the Bureau feels assured.

The district of Hawaii, with headquarters at Honolulu, is an important one in the administration of the laws. The report of the officer in charge is eminently satisfactory, and the fact that the laws are being enforced without friction in these islands, so far removed from our mainland and containing so large an oriental population, is of itself a tribute to the quality of the employees engaged in the work.

Although the other West India Islands contain a considerable Chinese population, Porto Rico constitutes a district of little importance, and even the Chinese of the exempt class do not avail themselves of either of the ports of entry there located—San Juan and Ponce.

14. Financial Statement.

The following table shows what it has cost the Government to administer the Chinese exclusion laws during the year:

Appropriation for enforcement of the Chinese exclusion act, 1906	$600,000.00
Disbursements on account of salaries and traveling expenses of inspectors, together with amount expended in the deportation of Chinese here in violation of law	400,523.36

This is a saving over the preceding year of $132,699.75, due principally to the fact that only half as many Chinese were deported, as shown by the following statement:

From the eastern Canadian border	10
From the western Canadian border	38
From the Mexican border	223
From other parts of the United States	39
Total	310

As will be seen from the accompanying financial statement, the total cost of making deportations was $27,882.81, an average cost of $89.94 for each Chinese person deported.

Expended for salaries and expenses of officers and miscellaneous items..	$372, 640. 55
Expended for deportation of prisoners entering the United States from the Canadian border	5, 500. 00
Expended for deportation of prisoners entering the United States from the Mexican border	17, 356. 91
Expended for deportation of prisoners entering the United States from other points	5, 025. 90

NOTE.—Fourteen Chinese have been deported, at an expense of $1,609.62, who are not included in the foregoing statement nor in the annual report for 1905, the expense of their deportation being payable from the appropriation for that fiscal year and they having been deported after the publication of said annual report.

The discrepancy between the preceding figures and those furnished by the fiscal representative of the Department of Commerce and Labor is explained by the fact that the former show the amount of vouchers approved for payment—some of which remain unpaid—while the latter represent actual disbursements from July 1, 1905, to June 30, 1906.

The Bureau, while not believing in a penurious policy when the accomplishment of results is desired, has always insisted that the utmost care be exercised in expending the funds appropriated for this object, and required that good reasons be shown for each such expenditure. The advisability of a change in the method of making the appropriation is described under subtitle 1 of this title (p. 77).

III. NATURALIZATION.

This title is a new one as representing a distinctive branch of the Bureau's work, although an examination of the reports for the past fiscal years will show that the subject has been regarded as of the greatest importance, not only to the prevention of undesirable immigration—for the deceit perpetrated in connection with gaining admission to this country by presenting fraudulent certificates of naturalization has for years been so extensive and persistent as to constitute a gigantic evil in itself—but also to an efficient protection of our nationality and civilization against the introduction of a wholly unprepared and unsuited, or actually vicious, alien element. The Bureau's views on the subject have therefore been expressed in no uncertain terms. It is but a mild indication of its feelings to say that it is gratified at the outcome of the labors of the commission appointed last summer by the President to investigate the subject and prepare a report and draft a bill for presentation to Congress, viz, the passage on the day preceding the close of the year covered by this report of a bill which, it is thought, will cure the evils that have accompanied and sprung from the careless and inefficient practices heretofore followed in conferring citizenship upon aliens. The year's work has confirmed and emphasized the views heretofore expressed as to the necessity for action of the character which Congress has taken, for with the added skill which is gained by experience the immigration officers have discovered in the hands of aliens of the inadmissible or undesirable classes during the year just closed numbers of fraudulent certificates of naturalization, and it has also been possible to render assistance to several of the United States attorneys in the prosecution and conviction of those guilty of originating such frauds. The following extract from the report of the commissioner at New York is quoted as an illustration:

In relation to some of the alleged naturalized Americans, it may be safely asserted that their personal appearance and grade of intelligence clearly indicate that their certificates of naturalization might properly have been withheld by the courts granting them, on the ground that the applicants for naturalization were not capable of intelligently appreciating the inestimable value of the citizenship thus conferred, or of exercising the great privileges it involves. The officers of this station have subjected all such alleged citizens to the very closest investigation, and have only admitted them as citizens on indubitable proof as to the validity of their respective claims. Of the total number of naturalization papers thus examined, 111 were thought to be fraudulently obtained or unlawfully held. The holders of such papers were taken in custody by a representative of the district attorney, and 96 convictions resulted. Those attempting to make unlawful use of them have been divested of their claims to citizenship, and 17 were sentenced to serve terms in the penitentiary; sentence was suspended in 44 cases, and fines aggregating $1,150 imposed in others. In the light of these deplorable facts, one finds genuine cause for exultation in the passage of an act by Congress specially designed to hedge about the granting of citizenship with much needed safeguards, which it is to be hoped will preclude the possibility of a recurrence of such cases.

Steps will immediately be taken to organize in the Bureau, which under the terms of the naturalization act is hereafter to be known as the "Bureau of Immigration and Naturalization," a division in direct charge of this most important enterprise upon which the General Government has embarked during recent years, and there is no hesitancy in predicting that by the date set in the bill for the inauguration throughout the country of the various details of the new plan of naturalization, viz, September 27, 1906, all arrangements will have been perfected. On the date of this report there is in contemplation the nomination, for the important position of chief of the new division, of Mr. Richard K. Campbell, who, by reason of his natural qualifications, his professional knowledge, and his long experience as an officer of the immigration service and legal adviser to the Bureau, added to his service on the commission which so thoroughly investigated the subject of naturalization and reported to the President the draft used as the basis of the measure finally passed by Congress, is probably the best equipped man available for the post.

IV. THE BUREAU OF IMMIGRATION.

1. Its Origin and Duties.

The Bureau of Immigration at Washington, the headquarters of the Immigration Service, had its origin in section 7 of the immigration act of March 3, 1891 (26 Stat., 1084), creating the office of the Superintendent of Immigration in the Treasury Department. That act provided that, in addition to the Superintendent of Immigration (the title was later changed to Commissioner-General of Immigration), there should be a chief clerk and two clerks in the office. The scope and character of the duties imposed upon the Bureau and its chief have been enormously increased with each addition to the immigration laws, and by the act of June 6, 1900 (31 Stat., 611), the enforcement of the Chinese exclusion laws was also vested in the Commissioner-General. To give any adequate or accurate description of the details of the Bureau's functions would require a document much more voluminous than this report, but the attempt is made to convey an idea of them by calling attention hereinafter to some of the more important items handled during the past year and by giving a brief account of the force of employees with which the work is accomplished and the systematic methods used to attain the maximum result with a minimum amount of labor and expense. The Immigration Service is spread all over the territory of the United States, is charged with varied and extensive duties, and engages over 1,200 employees. The affairs of this vast institution must be carefully supervised, and the efforts of the men must be directed and the results of their labors used so as to further the common cause of efficiently and economically enforcing the immigration, the alien contract labor, and the Chinese exclusion laws. That is the work in which the Bureau is constantly engaged.

2. Data Concerning Work of the Bureau.

The greater part of the supervising, harmonizing, and concentrating of the endeavors of its large force of field employees must, of course, be accomplished by the Bureau through written communications, entailing an enormous daily correspondence with its officers alone, to which there is added a correspondence of almost equal proportions with other branches of the Government and with private parties. The bare statement of the average number of letters of these classes received and sent daily would be inadequate as an indication of what is accomplished and of the work involved, therefore a few items of information concerning the different classes of cases covered by them are furnished as general illustrations of the scope and character of the Bureau's functions.

During the fiscal year just closed the evidence accompanying appeals from excluding decisions rendered at the various ports has been reviewed in the cases of 3,886 aliens and in the cases of 221 Chinese. These appeals involve the welfare of human beings and each item of the evidence—always voluminous in the Chinese cases and often so in the others—must be accorded its proper weight under the law invoked in each instance. After reviewing the evidence a summary thereof and an expression of the Bureau's opinion is submitted in each case, and upon the Department's approval or disapproval of such opinion a decision is prepared for the Secretary's signature. Throughout the United States approximately 700 aliens have been taken into custody on Department warrant, of which number 615 have been expelled from the country as being members of some one of the several classes prohibited by law from residing here after having failed at the hearing accorded them to rebut the evidence of unlawful residence on the strength of which the arrest had been ordered. Aside from the ordinary correspondence necessarily incident to the execution of these warrants—and in many cases the Bureau must direct an extended search for the alien—the evidence presented as a condition precedent to the issuance of the warrant of arrest, as well as that adduced at the hearing, must be accorded painstaking scrutiny to insure a proper application of the law in each instance, for such cases involve the rights of the alien, of the transportation company responsible for his presence in the United States, and, in a sense, even of the country from which the alien migrated. To effect the expulsion of these aliens from all parts of the country without giving just cause for complaint is a matter of some difficulty, requiring a nice and exact administration, especially as many of them are criminals, insane persons, or persons physically incapacitated. Separate bills on account of hospital care and maintenance and for transportation expenses in each of the said cases have been carefully examined and transmitted for collection from the various transportation companies responsible. Thorough investigation of the claims of various public institutions in reference to alien inmates thereof has necessitated the issuance by the Bureau of separate authorizations for hospital treatment in the cases of 732 aliens.

Approximately 1,525 letters authorizing expenditures for quarters, services, and supplies have been prepared and issued by the Bureau with the Department's approval, as well as nearly 500 contracts for like purposes. Miscellaneous vouchers, pay rolls, head tax, and other accounts, to the number of over 15,000, have been reviewed by comparative and checking methods and appropriately entered in the Bureau's permanent records; while 198 letters imposing fines on steamship companies, which fines aggregate $24,300, have been prepared for the Department's approval after investigating and considering the evidence obtained.

Emergencies to which the service is normally subject render the granting of extended leaves of absence to employees almost impracticable; hence it has been necessary to consider, record, and respond to over 3,000 individual requests for such leaves during the period covered by this report. With rare exception it has been impracticable, if not unnecessary, to make written replies to over 4,000 requests for the statistical and other publications of the Bureau, which requests have, however, been promptly complied with by furnishing the documents called for. Requests for official badges, insignia, uniform caps, fountain pens, and accessories to the number of 516 have had attention, the writing of one or more letters, in addition to the keeping of accounts, being necessary in each instance.

The Bureau now compiles its own statistics from monthly reports forwarded by the field officers. The summaries of those statistics, contained in the tables and charts of this report, do not furnish even an outline of the tedious details of this undertaking.

There are now in the files of the Bureau, arranged methodically and conveniently, all of the records relating to the registration of Chinese formerly filed in the offices of the various collectors of internal revenue and collectors of customs throughout the country. The certificate of every laborer who leaves the country with the intention of returning must be compared with said records before his papers can be approved, in addition to which comparisons are constantly being made with a view to detect forgeries and frauds perpetrated in connection with the issuance of counterfeit or changed certificates. The Bureau has also, after considering the evidence submitted and consulting the said records to confirm or refute such evidence, acted upon applications for certificates of residence to the extent and in the manner indicated by the following table:

APPLICATIONS FOR CERTIFICATES OF RESIDENCE DURING THE FISCAL YEAR ENDED JUNE 30, 1906.

Cases pending from previous year	113	
Cases reopened	10	
Applications received	137	
		260
Duplicate certificates issued	149	
Original certificates issued	4	
Original certificates found	4	
New photographs affixed to certificates	1	
Applications denied	29	
Cases dropped	40	
Cases pending	33	
		260

For purposes of comparison see table, page 88 of the annual report for 1905.

The foregoing are only some of the more important items handled during the course of the year, all of which require the examination of evidence, a general knowledge of legal principles, and a thorough understanding of the immigration and Chinese exclusion laws, regulations, and decisions, or a technical acquaintance with accounting, statistical, and correspondence methods and practices. In disposing of the vast majority of the matters which come before the Bureau each case must be considered on its individual merits, and anything partaking in the least of the formal or perfunctory must be avoided.

As a general comprehensive statement, it might be said that the Bureau's files show the issuance during the year of considerably over 28,000 original communications of a nature requiring study, care, and technical knowledge in the preparation, to which must be added a much greater number of references, indorsements, and formal approvals and acknowledgments, all of which must be signed by the chief of the Bureau.

A conservative estimate is that the work accomplished during 1905 has been three times as great as that for 1903, the last year of the Bureau's connection with the Treasury Department. While this immense increase is due partly to the growth of immigration, and the consequent addition to the service at large, the extent of such increase is so far from bearing an exact ratio to the advance in immigration that we must look elsewhere for a full explanation. It is this: As the years have added to the experience of the Bureau, it has been possible, by the extension of its already existing plans and the adoption of additional methods, to bring the entire service at large more completely under its control and to exercise a much more detailed supervision over the affairs of such service. This has produced a very considerable saving of time and money. Thus, instances exist where, under plans in use a few years ago, the services of two inspectors would be required, one man will now do the same work quite as effectively; and so, in varying degree, throughout every part of the service, personal or material. In the ultimate, therefore, this increase in the duties of the Bureau, which standing alone looms large, is inconsiderable by comparison with the general saving accomplished. Moreover, as will appear from the information given under the next subtitle, the increase in the size of the Bureau and its force of employees has been wholly disproportionate to the additions to its duties brought about in the two ways above mentioned.

3. Its Methods and Personnel.

The Bureau of Immigration is thoroughly, systematically, and practically organized—is a business institution, conducted under modern business methods. It has gradually gathered to itself a corps of officers and clerks, which for the intelligence, devotion to duty, and wide-awake activity of its members could not be surpassed, and is seldom equaled in any branch of business, public or private. This is due in part to good fortune, but largely to the exercise of care in making selections of employees. At the date of this report the Bureau is manned as follows: The Commissioner-General; the chief clerk and actuary, who acts as Commissioner-General when the chief of the Bureau is absent; the chief of the correspondence division, who acts as chief clerk in the absence of the latter, an assistant chief, and 6 clerks and stenographers; the chief of the Chinese record division and 1 assistant; the chief of the immigration record division and 1 assistant; the chief of the accounts division and 4 assistants; the chief of the statistical division and 1 assistant; the law officer; the confidential clerk to the Commissioner-General; 2 messengers, and an assistant messenger. Thus it will be seen that the headquarters of the entire Immigration Service is conducted with a force, all told, of 25 persons. So thoroughly organized is this body of faithful employees, and so complete is every detail of the system under which it labors, that, while each officer is a specialist in some particular branch of the Bureau's functions, they are, with the exception of those engaged upon wholly dissimilar duties, brought into such contact with other branches of the work that a practical knowledge of each part is obtained by all, thus lending an unusual elasticity to the force and preventing any waste of time or energy. This combining of specialization and generalization is what makes possible the accomplishment of so much by so small a force. Yet the details of administration are so arranged that all matters of importance receive the personal attention of the chief executive officer and of the Commissioner-General himself. The reins of control are firmly but kindly held at all times, belief being strong in the principle that more is accomplished by treating the employees as men of honor than by regarding them as mere tools. The Bureau has an advantage over some other branches of the Government in the fact that its work is of a live, current nature. Each employee is able to feel that he is individually responsible for the part he is taking in the solution of the problem of controlling immigration; that the impress of his personal endeavors is left upon the work—resulting in the exhibition of a lively interest by each officer in all the affairs of the Service. Under these circumstances, although required to labor more assiduously than the average Government employee, they are more than content with their lot, and both approach and leave their desks daily in that cheerful frame of mind which conduces so largely to the character of work performed and to the health and welfare of those engaged therein.

The systems of keeping records, preparing correspondence, reviewing accounts, and compiling statistics are as complete and, at the same time, as simple as can be devised. The correspondence, involving as it naturally does, an intricacy of subjects practically without limit, must be effectively indexed and filed, to the end that it may readily be referred to. When the flexibility of the names and titles involved is considered, the difficulties encountered, but successfully overcome, in these respects can be appreciated. Its business is transacted on time, no accumulations of work being permitted. The Bureau's capacity in the respects mentioned has been tried to the utmost limit in the past year, and has stood the strain.

V. RECOMMENDATIONS REGARDING ADDITIONAL LEGISLATION.

The Bureau regrets that Senate bill No. 4403, introduced near the close of the last session, did not become law, owing to the volume of business then before both Houses of Congress, for the hands of the Service would have been materially strengthened by its provisions. It contained many of the more important suggestions advanced in last year's report (pp. 75–78) regarding additional restrictions upon the immigration of aliens. Attention is again called to those suggestions in the hope that they may be considered by Congress at its next session. The same or additional reasons for urging them now exist, many of which reasons are stated incidentally in the preceding pages of this report. The following is a summary of the recommendations advanced in both reports, with reference to the pages thereof, respectively, where the need is explained in detail; also of the recommendations regarding changes in the Chinese exclusion laws arranged in the same manner:

IMMIGRATION.

Recommendation.	1905 report.	1906 report.
	Page.	*Page.*
1. That legislation be adopted to check violations of the immigration laws by professed seamen; penalizing ship-masters for signing other than bona fide seamen on their crew lists; requiring them to notify immigration officers of the arrival of vessels with aliens in the crew, and to prevent the escape into the United States of any member of such crew declared by the immigration officers to be inadmissible	77	57
2. That Public Health and Marine-Hospital surgeons be stationed at the principal foreign ports of embarkation to examine all aliens applying for passage to the United States, and thus aid in the prevention of the sale of passage to any who, under the United States immigration laws, can not be permitted to enter this country	47, 75	63–64
3. In the event that, for any reason, recommendation No. 2 can not be adopted, the fine of $100 now imposed by section 2 of the immigration act of March 3, 1903, upon steamship companies for bringing to ports of this country aliens afflicted with dangerous or loathsome contagious diseases which could have been detected by competent medical inspection prior to embarkation, be increased to $500, with a view to compelling the transportation companies to adopt effective measures on this subject; and that such penalty be extended to cover the bringing of insane or weak-minded persons, idiots, and imbeciles	75–76	62–63
4. That a comprehensive digest of existing legislation on the subject of immigration be published in the principal foreign languages and extensively distributed abroad, for the purpose of educating foreign peoples concerning the difficulties which are placed in the way of immigration to the United States	77–78	64
5. That an appropriate measure be adopted under which the various sections of the United States that need foreign settlers may be enabled to place before the immigrants arriving at the principal seaports of this country, particularly at Ellis Island, a statement and illustrations regarding the inducements offered settlers by such sections	58	65
6. That the President's suggestion of last year for the closing of the Mexican border to all aliens, except citizens of Mexico, be adopted	....	69
7. That the buildings now used as an immigrant station on Ellis Island, New York Harbor, be remodeled throughout, so as to properly adapt them to the conduct of the large and ever-increasing business of examining arriving aliens	....	70–71
8. That, unless some interested transportation company can be induced to erect at Philadelphia a suitable building for use as an immigrant station, the Government purchase a proper site and erect such a station itself	....	71

IMMIGRATION—Continued.

Recommendation.	1905 report.	1906 report.
	Page.	*Page.*
9. That some further legislation be enacted to strengthen the hands of the Government in such a manner as to make it possible to more effectively punish individuals and corporations that induce aliens to come to this country under promise or assurance of employment; particularly with regard to the establishment of rules of evidence in these cases	45, 76	65-66
10. That the provisions of law which, for the first time in 1903, after twenty-one years' continuous practice to the contrary, abolished the head tax on account of alien passengers intending to land at our ports for transit through the United States to some foreign country, be repealed	77	
11. That to obviate difficulties of administration, any alien who has been domiciled in Canada or Mexico for more than one year be exempt, when entering the United States, from the payment of head tax, in the same manner as are citizens of those countries	77	
12. That the masters of vessels be required, as a condition precedent to obtaining clearance papers from ports of this country, to furnish to the immigration officers lists or manifests of outgoing alien passengers on such vessel, prepared and verified in like manner as the manifests or lists of arriving aliens	77	
13. As a means of preventing a further increase of alien immigration it will be necessary, if such a policy is deemed expedient, either to enlarge the prohibited classes by adding thereto those who are illiterate; those whom age or feebleness renders incapable of self-support, if at all, but temporarily and under the most favorable conditions; all children under 17 years of age unaccompanied by their parents, unless coming to join parents already in this country who are able to support them, or unless in the case of death of both parents they are coming to join brothers or sisters or uncles or aunts already in the United States who are willing and able to support them, and will furnish proper security therefor; those who have not brought a sufficient sum of money to enable them to maintain themselves for a reasonable time in the event of sickness or temporary lack of employment; or else to adopt adequate means, enforced by sufficient penalties, to compel steamship companies engaged in the passenger business to observe in good faith the law which forbids them to encourage or solicit immigration to the United States. If all other means are found ineffective it might not be unwise to borrow a device of the Canadian laws which has long been used as an effective check on Chinese immigration—a limitation upon vessels coming to its ports, apportioning the number of such passengers in a direct ratio to the tonnage of such vessels	49, 57, 76	60-61
14. In addition to the thirteen recommendations given above it is urged that an international conference be held on the subjects of immigration and emigration, an effort being made to induce all interested countries to send delegates to such convention with the object of arranging a plan of cooperation whereby the immigration laws of this country may be more effectively administered, and the hardship and suffering to subjects of other countries, who proceed to our ports only to find that they can not enter and must return to their former homes, may be obviated or overcome	78	61

CHINESE EXCLUSION.

Recommendation.	1905 report.	1906 report.
1. Congress having, in making the last appropriation for the enforcement of the Chinese exclusion laws, stipulated that the amount so expended shall be drawn from the immigrant fund, it is recommended that when the next appropriation is made the language thereof be such as to authorize the payment of all expenses incident to the enforcement of the Chinese exclusion laws from the same appropriation and in the same manner as the expenses of regulating immigration, and that the designation of all Chinese inspectors be changed to immigrant inspectors, the object being to effectuate a complete combination of the two branches of the service, which would conduce greatly to the economy and efficiency of administration as well as remove some real and imaginary causes for complaint		77-78
2. That section 6 of the act approved July 5, 1884, be amended so as to authorize the stationing in China of officers directly responsible to the Department of Commerce and Labor to discharge the duty of investigating and approving certificates issued by the Chinese Government to members of the exempt classes; such officers to be attached to the United States consulates	97-98	83-85
3. That a provision be incorporated in the exclusion laws under which the minor children of domiciled members of the exempt classes may be admitted to the United States solely for the purpose of joining their parent or parents and for engagement in the exempt pursuits, the purpose being to prevent the introduction and residence here of members of the laboring class who secure admission as minor children		86
4. That all restrictions on the departure and return of registered Chinese laborers be removed, so that such persons may leave and reenter the United States merely upon establishing their identity	98-99	86-87

CHINESE EXCLUSION—Continued.

Recommendation.	1905 report.	1906 report.
	Page.	*Page.*
5. That all Chinese now in the United States be registered, under a complete and detailed plan, irrespective of whether they registered under the acts of 1892 and 1893	100	87–88
6. That the method of arresting and deporting Chinese found unlawfully in the United States be changed so as to correspond with the plan now so successfully operated with regard to aliens of all other races	99	88
7. That, unless the desired object can be accomplished by departmental regulations, legislative authority be given for the taking up at ports of entry of the certificates issued to members of the exempt classes under section 6 of the act of July 5, 1884, issuing in lieu thereof a durable identification card incapable of being counterfeited	....	88–89
8. That the provisions of law regarding Chinese seamen be so amended as to attach a definitely fixed, severe penalty to the permitting of the landing of such seamen, irrespective of whether the officers of a vessel connive in the landing, a more severe penalty being provided in case of connivance upon their part	....	93
9. That appropriate legislation be passed to remove all doubt with regard to how the deck of an American vessel is to be considered under the Chinese exclusion and alien contract-labor laws	100	93

VI. CONCLUSION.

It is believed that this year's report, like all the preceding ones, demonstrates that the Immigration Service is progressive. Each year, despite the added burdens naturally resulting from the steady increase in immigration, it has moved forward at least a few steps toward the attainment of the ideal. This general progress is the sum of the efforts of each one of the intelligent, efficient officers who forms a part of its large force. The combining of these endeavors into a harmonious whole is due primarily to the executive ability and earnest, honest work of the commissioners and inspectors in charge, and finally to the supervision exercised by the Bureau itself. Too high terms of commendation can not be used in speaking of the individual employees of the Immigration Service and of the Public Health and Marine-Hospital surgeons who assist them in the work of guarding our gates against the entry of the vicious and diseased that are so ready to come and of whom other countries are so willing to be rid. Their devotion to duty is the basis of the success that has been attained. With better weapons we who constitute the Service could have fought a better battle; but much has been accomplished—we have done the best we could.

Respectfully,

F. P. SARGENT,
Commissioner-General.

The SECRETARY OF COMMERCE AND LABOR.

INDEX.

Page.

Accommodations of outward-bound passengers 50
Administrative work of Bureau of Immigration 100
Admitted. *See* Aliens admitted.
Advertising for immigrants, ineffectiveness of law prohibiting 61
Africa, alien arrivals from. *See* Charts.
Ages of immigrants 6
  See also Aliens admitted; Passenger movement.
Alien contract laborers. *See* Contract laborers.
Alien seamen deserting at American ports. 57
Alien stowaways arriving at various ports. 57
Aliens, arrivals and rejections in 1906 .... 3, 49
  classification of arrivals 4
  disposition of appeals 58, 59
  ethnic character of arrivals. *See* Charts.
  physical and mental condition of arriving 61
  problems concerning distribution 64
  problems concerning sources 59
  who constitute immigrant and nonimmigrant, and transits 4
  See also Chinese.
Aliens admitted, ages, sex, literacy, and financial condition, by races or peoples, 1906 .... 6, 8
  by countries, showing increase or decrease, 1905 and 1906 6
  by countries and races or peoples, 1906 .. 17
  by decades and countries, 1861-1906 40
  by destinations and occupations, 1906 .. 34
  by destinations and races or peoples, 1906 23
  by months and sex, 1905 and 1906 16
  by occupations and races or peoples, 1906 28
  by ports and sex, 1905 and 1906 5
  by sex and countries, January 1 to December 31, 1905 42
    July 1 to December 31, 1905 44
    July 1, 1905, to June 30, 1906 22
    January 1 to June 30, 1906 45
  by years, 1820-1906 43
    1892-1906 14
  efforts to distribute 64
  immigrant and nonimmigrant, by ports, 1906 49
  nonimmigrant, by countries of final destination and last permanent residence, 1906 .... 45, 46

Page.

Aliens admitted, number who had been in United States before 8, 49
  See also Charts; Chinese, statistical tables.
Aliens debarred, by ports, 1906 49
  by ports and causes (citizens of foreign contiguous territory), 1906 .... 14, 15
  by races or peoples and causes, 1906 10
  number and causes, 1904-1906 7
    1892-1906 14
  See also Charts; Chinese, statistical tables.
Aliens deported, January 1 to June 30, 1906, by races or peoples and causes 12-13
  See also Chinese, statistical tables.
Aliens relieved in hospital, by races or peoples, in 1906 10
Aliens returned after landing, 1892-1906 14
  by races or peoples, 1906 .... 7, 10
  See also Charts; Chinese, statistical tables.
Angel Island, Cal., new immigrant station. 71
Appeals from decisions under immigration laws 58, 59
  See also Chinese, statistical tables.
Areas of racial grand divisions of Europe. *See* Charts.
Arrivals. *See* Aliens.
Asia, alien arrivals from. *See* Aliens; Charts; Chinese.
Attorney-General, opinion relative to alien contract laborers .... 67, footnote

Baltimore, decrease in arrivals 4, 5
  report of commissioner 73
Borders, conditions along Canadian and Mexican 68, 93
Boston, decrease in arrivals 4, 5
  report of Chinese inspector 97
  report of commissioner 72
British Isles, decreased immigration 5, 6, 59
Bureau of Immigration, administrative work 100

California, report of Chinese inspector 96
Canada, citizens of, debarred, and causes.. 14, 15
  conditions along border 68, 93
  immigrants admitted through 5
  inward passenger movement through.. 49
  Japanese immigration through 67
  jurisdiction of commissioner of immigration 68
  report of commissioner 68, 73
  See also Chinese, discussion.

Page.

Causes, for debarring aliens........... 7, 10, 14, 15
for deporting aliens..................... 12-13
Certificates of identification proposed for exempt classes of Chinese................ 88
Charts, explanations........,.... 4, 14, 21, 27, 40, 43
Chart 1. Proportion of arrivals at seaports debarred from landing, and proportion of landed afterwards returned; number debarred, and causes therefor; number returned after landing, and number of arrivals, 1892-1906.................................facing 14
Chart 2. Races and countries of last permanent residence of immigrants, 1906..,..............................facing 20
Chart 3. Proportion of immigration and number of immigrants going to each State, 1906...........................facing 26
Chart 4. Per cent of immigration for last eight years to each State and Territory, by race.......................facing 26
Chart 5. Per cent of total immigration to each State, 1892-1906...........facing 40
Chart 6. Per cent of immigrants arrived in last eight years, in each occupation group, by States and Territories, ...facing 40
Chart 7. Wave of immigration into the United States from all countries, 1820-1906...................................facing 42
Children of domiciled Chinese merchants, identification.............................. 86
China, stationing of immigration officers in. 85
Chinese, admissions of native-born........ 90
admissions of transit.................. 92
discussion relating to exclusion........ 75
employment as seamen................ 92
identification of exempt classes..... 85, 86, 88
importations of slave girls and prostitutes................................... 91
new registration proposed.............. 87
receipts and disbursements in enforcement of exclusion laws............... 98
recommendations concerning exclusion.. 77, 106
reports of inspectors,.................... 90
"section 6" exempt classes............ 83
special report to Congress regarding enforcement of exclusion laws......... 76
statistical tables....................... 78-83
See also Aliens debarred, etc.
Classification of alien arrivals.............. 4
Cold-storage plant at Ellis Island, recommendation concerning................... 70
Colonization of immigrants, efforts to prevent.. 65
Commissioner of immigration for Canada, jurisdiction............................... 68
Commissioners of immigration, reports.... 72
Conference, international, on immigration and emigration, recommended........... 61
Congress, special report to, relating to enforcement of Chinese-exclusion laws..... 76
Consuls, examination of Chinese by........ 83, 84
Contagious diseases among immigrants increasing.................................. 61
See also Aliens debarred.

Contiguous territory, citizens debarred, and causes... 14, 15
Contract laborers, efforts to prevent importation.................................... 65
opinion of Attorney-General..... 67, footnote
See also Aliens debarred.
Countries contributing immigrants........ 59
See also Aliens admitted.
Crimes, etc. *See* Aliens debarred.

Debarred. *See* Aliens debarred.
Decades, immigration by. *See* Aliens admitted.
Decisions under immigration laws, disposition of appeals from.................. 58, 59
See also Chinese, statistical tables.
Definition of "poor physique"............. 62
Denmark, decreased immigration.......... 5, 6, 59
Deported. *See* Aliens deported.
Depression in immigration, periods........ 43
Desertions of alien seamen................. 57
Destinations of immigrants, problems concerning............................... 64
unreliability of statistics concerning... 16
See also Aliens admitted; Charts.
Destinations of outward-bound passengers. 50
Diseases among immigrants, increase in contagious............................ 61
See also Aliens debarred.
Disposition of appeals under immigration laws.. 58, 59
See also Chinese, statistical tables.
Dissatisfied laboring classes, immigration. 60
Distribution of aliens, problems concerning.. 64
Division of Naturalization, organization... 99
Domiciled Chinese, identification........... 85, 86
Duties devolving upon Bureau of Immigration.. 100

Eastern Europe, increased immigration.. 5, 6, 59
El Paso, admissions of Chinese....... 86, 91, 94, 95
new immigrant station...... 72
report of inspector................. 69
Ellis Island, facilities and needs............ 69
report of commissioner................ 72
England, decreased immigration.......... 5, 6, 59
Ethnic character of alien arrivals. *See* Aliens admitted, etc.; Charts.
Europe, alien arrivals by racial grand divisions. *See* Charts.
increased immigration from eastern and southern.......................... 5, 6, 59
Examination abroad of prospective immigrants...................................... 63
Exclusion of Chinese. *See* Chinese.
Exempt classes of Chinese under section 6. 83
Expenditures, statements of receipts and.. 74, 98

Facilities at immigrant stations........... 69
Females admitted. *See* Aliens admitted.
Ferryboat recommended for Ellis Island .. 71
Financial condition of immigrants........ 6, 8
Financial statements........................ 74, 98
Fines, collected from steamship companies. 62
ineffectiveness of steamship............ 63
recommendations concerning......... 63
Foreign contiguous territory, citizens of, debarred, and causes..................... 14, 15

Page.

Galveston, increase in arrivals ... 4, 5
new immigrant station ... 71
Germany, decreased immigration ... 5, 6, 59
Great Britain, decreased immigration ... 5, 6, 59
Greece, increased immigration ... 5, 6, 60
Grounds for debarring aliens. *See* Aliens debarred.

Hawaii, Japanese immigration through ... 66
report of Chinese inspector ... 98
See also Honolulu.
Hebrews, increased immigration ... 60
History of Bureau of Immigration ... 100
Honolulu, decrease in arrivals ... 4, 5
See also Hawaii.
Hospital aid to aliens ... 7, 11
Hospital at Ellis Island, recommendation concerning ... 70

Identification. *See* Chinese.
Idiocy among immigrants increasing ... 61
See also Aliens debarred.
Illiteracy of immigrants ... 6, 8
Immigrant aliens. *See* Aliens; Aliens admitted.
Immigrant inspectors. *See* Inspectors.
Immigrant stations, facilities and needs ... 69
Immigrants, efforts to distribute ... 64
nativities, destinations, occupations, sex, etc. *See* Aliens; Aliens admitted.
Immigration, administrative work of Bureau of ... 100
by countries, destinations, occupations, ports, races or peoples, sex, etc. *See* Aliens admitted.
commissioners of, reports ... 72
discussion concerning ... 3
international conference recommended 61
periods of depression ... 43
problems concerning sources and distribution ... 59, 64
wave of, since 1820. *See* Charts.
See also Aliens admitted.
Immigration inspectors. *See* Inspectors.
Immigration laws, publication abroad ... 64
Immigration officers, stationing in China recommended ... 85
Importations of contract laborers ... 65
Increase in immigration ... 3
Inducements to immigration ... 59
Insanity among immigrants increasing ... 61
See also Aliens debarred.
Inspection abroad of prospective immigrants, defective ... 63
Inspection work of officers ... 4
Inspectors in charge, reports of ... 72, 96
International conference on immigration and emigration, recommended ... 61
Inward passenger movement, by ports ... 49
Ireland, decreased emigration ... 5, 6, 59
Italy, increased immigration ... 5, 6, 60

Japanese immigration ... 66
Jurisdiction of commissioner of immigration for Canada ... 68

Key West, decrease in arrivals ... 4, 5

Page.

Laborers, identification of domiciled Chinese ... 86
See also Contract laborers.
Laboring classes, immigration of dissatisfied ... 60
Laws, immigration, evaded by deserting seamen ... 57
publication abroad ... 64
Legislation recommended ... 105
Lines of steamships, outward passenger movement over various ... 50
Literacy. *See* Illiteracy.

Males admitted. *See* Aliens admitted.
Malone, N. Y., report of Chinese inspector. 97
Medical inspection abroad of aliens ... 63
Medical officers abroad, stationing recommended ... 63
Mental condition of arriving aliens ... 61
Merchants, identification of domiciled Chinese, and their wives and children ... 85, 86
Mexico, citizens of, debarred, and causes ... 14, 15
conditions along border ... 68, 93, 98
contract-labor immigration ... 67
Minor children of Chinese domiciled merchants, identification ... 86
Money brought by immigrants ... 6, 8
Money sent out of the United States by aliens ... 7
Monthly statement of aliens admitted, 1905 and 1906, by sex ... 16
Montreal, report of commissioner ... 68

Native-born Chinese, admissions ... 90
Nativity of aliens admitted, debarred, deported, and relieved in hospitals. *See* Aliens admitted, etc.
Naturalization Division, organization ... 99
New England, fraudulent immigration of Chinese ... 76
report of Chinese inspector ... 97
New Orleans, decrease in arrivals ... 4, 5
new immigrant station ... 71
report of Chinese inspector ... 97
New York, increased arrivals ... 4, 5
report of Chinese Inspector ... 97
Nonimmigrant aliens. *See* Aliens; Aliens admitted.
Northern Europe, decreased immigration. 5, 6, 59
Northwest, Japanese laborers for railroads. 66

Occupations of immigrants, unreliability of statistics concerning ... 16
See also Aliens admitted; Charts.
Opinion of Attorney-General relative to alien contract laborers ... 67, footnote
Oregon, report of Chinese inspector ... 96
Origin of Bureau of Immigration ... 100
Outward passenger movement, by ports of departure and destination, 1906 ... 50
total by years, 1890–1906 ... 56

Passenger movement, inward, by ports ... 49
outward, by ages, sex, lines of vessels, ports of departure and destination, and classes of accommodation ... 50

Page.
Pauperism, etc. *See* Aliens debarred.
Peoples admitted, debarred, deported, and treated in hospitals. *See* Aliens admitted, etc.; Charts.
Periods of depression in immigration...... 43
Personnel of Bureau of Immigration...... 104
Philadelphia, decrease in arrivals.......... 4, 5
report of Chinese inspector............ 97
report of commissioner................ 73
Physical condition of aliens.............. 61
Physicians, stationing abroad recommended.................................. 63
Physique, definition of poor............... 62
Port Townsend, report of Chinese inspector..................................... 97
transfer of immigrant station to Seattle. 71
Portal, N. Dak., report of Chinese inspector. 97
Portland, Me., new immigrant station..... 71
Portland, Oreg., report Chinese inspector.. 96
Porto Rico, report of commissioner at San Juan.. 73
Ports, aliens admitted, debarred, etc., by. *See* Aliens admitted, etc.
disposition of appeals of aliens at various.................................... 58
fines collected at various................ 62
inward passenger movement through various.................................. 49
outward-bound passenger movement through and to various............... 50
receipts and expenditures at various... 74
stowaways arrived at various........... 57
Problems, distribution of aliens............ 64
sources of and inducements to immigration.................................... 59
Professional occupations of immigrants. *See* Aliens admitted; Charts.
Proportion of aliens admitted, debarred, and returned for fifteen years. *See* Charts.
Proportion of immigrants going to various States. *See* Charts.
Prosperity reflected in immigration........ 43
Prostitutes, importations of Chinese........ 91
See also Aliens debarred.
Public charges, proportion, for fifteen years, of aliens returned after becoming. *See* Charts.
Publication abroad of immigration laws... 64

Races of aliens admitted, debarred, deported, returned, and treated in hospital. *See* Aliens admitted, etc.; Charts.
Railroads, immigrant contract labor for southwestern........................... 67
Japanese labor imported for northwestern.................................. 66
Receipts and expenditures, statements of.. 74, 98
Recommendations regarding legislation... 105
Refrigerating plant at Ellis Island, recommendation concerning................... 70
Registration of Chinese, proposed......... 87
Rejected. *See* Aliens debarred.
Relieved in hospital, number and races or peoples of aliens.......................... 7, 11
Returned. *See* Aliens returned.
Richford, Vt., report of Chinese inspector. 97
Russia, increased immigration........... 5, 6, 60

Page.
Sailors, desertions of alien................. 57
employment of Chinese................ 92
San Francisco, decrease in arrivals........ 4, 5
decreased Japanese immigration....... 67
new immigrant station at Angel Island 71
report of commissioner................. 73
report of Chinese inspector............. 96
San Juan, P. R., report of commissioner... 73
Scotland, decreased immigration......... 5, 6, 59
Seamen, desertions of alien................ 57
employment of Chinese................ 92
Seaports. *See* Ports.
Seattle, new immigrant station............ 71
"Section 6" exempt classes of Chinese..... 83
Sex. *See* Aliens admitted; Passenger movement.
Skilled occupations of immigrants. *See* Aliens admitted; Charts.
Slave girls, importations of Chinese........ 91
Smuggling of Chinese. *See* Chinese.
Sources of immigration.................... 5, 6, 59
See also Aliens admitted.
Southern States, immigrants sought by.... 64
Southern Europe, increased immigration. 5, 6, 59
Southwest, immigration of contract labor.. 67
States, destinations of immigrants, by. *See* Aliens admitted; Charts.
immigrants sought by Southern....... 64
Stations at which aliens were admitted, debarred, etc. *See* Aliens admitted, etc.; Immigrant stations; Ports.
Statistical tables, Chinese................... 78
explanation............................. 4
Steamship lines, fines collected............ 62
inducements offered immigrants....... 60
recommendation concerning fines..... 68
outward passenger movement over various................................ 50
Stowaways arriving at various ports....... 57
Sumas, Wash., report of Chinese inspector. 97
Surgeons, stationing abroad recommended. 63
Supervising Architect of the Treasury, inspection of buildings at Ellis Island...... 70
Sweden, decreased immigration.......... 5, 6, 59

Tables, Chinese statistical.................. 78
explanation of charts and statistical... 4
Trachoma, dangerous character........... 62
Trades of immigrants. *See* Aliens admitted; Charts.
Transits, admissions of Chinese............ 92
who constitute.......................... 4
See also Aliens; Aliens admitted.
Transportation companies. *See* Steamship lines.
Treated in hospital, aliens.................. 10
Turkey, increased immigration............ 5, 6, 60

United Kingdom, decreased immigration. 5, 6, 59

Washington, report of Chinese inspectors. 97
Wave of immigration since 1820. *See* Charts.
Western Europe, decreased immigration.. 5, 6, 59
Western Hemisphere, alien arrivals. *See* Charts.
Wives of domiciled Chinese merchants, identification............................ 86
Work of Bureau of Immigration............ 100

O

www.ingramcontent.com/pod-product-compliance
Lightning Source LLC
Chambersburg PA
CBHW030629270326
41927CB00007B/1372

* 9 7 8 3 7 4 1 1 4 0 8 5 3 *